Alternative Investment Operations

Jason Scharfman

Alternative Investment Operations

Hedge Funds, Private Equity, and Fund of Funds

palgrave
macmillan

Jason Scharfman
Corgentum Consulting, LLC
New York, NY, USA

ISBN 978-3-030-46628-2   ISBN 978-3-030-46629-9   (eBook)
https://doi.org/10.1007/978-3-030-46629-9

This Palgrave Macmillan imprint is published by the registered company Springer Nature Switzerland AG.
The registered company address is: Gewerbestrasse 11, 6330 Cham, Switzerland

This book is dedicated to my entire family for their continued support

Preface

Alternative investments such as hedge funds, private equity and fund of funds continue to be of strong interest among the investment community. As these investment strategies have become increasingly complex, fund managers have continued to devote more time and resources toward developing best practice operations to support the actual trade processing, fund accounting and back-office mechanics that allow these strategies to function. Representatives of this operational growth estimates have indicated that fund managers have seen increased operating budgets of 30% or more in recent years. As a result, it is now more important than ever for those that work in any aspect of the alternative investment industry to develop and maintain an understanding of the key aspects of fund operations.

To provide an overview of different aspects of important alternative investment fund operations, this book is structured intro three sections. The first section, Chaps. 1, 2, 3, and 4, provides an introduction to core alternative investment fund operations. Topics covered in this section include trade operations, cash management oversight and compliance operations. The second section of the book, Chaps. 5, 6, 7, and 8, expands the analysis to include the role of third parties in the alternative investment space. This section begins with a discussion on the role of services providers such as fund administrators and consultants. It continues with an overview of information technology operations and operational risk management considerations.

The third and final section of the book, Chaps. 9, 10, 11, and 12, focuses on more specific operational considerations. This section begins by providing an overview of the unique operational considerations of private equity and fund of funds. It continues by discussing considerations for documenting operational policies and procedures. Next, techniques for ongoing testing, training and surveillance of fund operations are presented. Finally, the book concludes by providing an overview of the techniques for the analysis of fund operations as well as a discussion of future trends in the space.

The best investment strategy in the world cannot be implemented without strong operations. By developing a thorough understanding of the core concepts of fund operations, investors, investment professionals, other fund personnel and fund service providers can ensure that operational risks are best mitigated and that the investment function will not be dragged down by poor operations, but rather supported and encouraged by it to realize profitable investments.

New York, NY   Jason Scharfman

Contents

List of Figures

List of Tables

1

Introduction to Alternative Investment Operations

Introduction

The term *alternative investments* lacks a single universally accepted definition. Additionally, there is not a uniform legal or regulatory definition for the term. There has been debate about even whether or not alternative investments are their own distinct asset class or rather a subset of existing asset classes. Others take the position that alternative investments are indeed their own separate asset class. Regardless of which position you take, alternative investments are generally classified into five types: commodity and managed futures, credit derivatives, corporate governance, hedge funds and private equity.[1]

In this book, we will classify hedge funds and private equity not as direct alternative investments themselves, but as types of *fund managers*. At its most basic level, a fund manager is a type of investment structure whereby investors give capital (i.e. money) to an individual to invest on their behalf. Alternatively, the term "fund manager" can also be used to refer to an entire firm consisting of multiple individuals and entities that manage capital. In practice, a number of different terms are utilized interchangeably with term "fund manager." For the purposes of this text, we will employ these conventions as well and a fund manager may also be referred to as an alternative investment firm, alternative investment fund, capital management firm, fund management firm or simply a firm.

Fund managers usually adhere to specific investment strategies. Hedge funds and private equity fund managers adhere to certain alternative

© The Author(s) 2020
J. Scharfman, *Alternative Investment Operations*,
https://doi.org/10.1007/978-3-030-46629-9_1

investment strategies. In this way, hedge funds and private equity can be thought of as having a dual role both as alternative investments themselves and, more practically, as fund managers of capital that allocate to alternative investment strategies. Alternative investment can be distinguished from the so-called *traditional investments* such as long-only mutual funds.

Classifying Fund Manager Activities

The functions of an alternative investments firm can be widely classified into two categories. The first category would be the investing activities of the firm. The investment function is typically led by an individual holding the title of *Chief Investment Officer* or *Portfolio Manager*. In many cases, investment decisions at alternative investment firms are reviewed by a group of investment professionals within a firm known as an investment committee. The investment-related tasks performed by the investment function include developing and managing the following:

- The investment strategies of the funds managed
- The investment theses behind the implementation of those investment strategies
- Investment risk management framework and restrictions applied

The second category, and the focus of this book, is the operational activities of the fund manager. Broadly, operational activities can be defined as everything else not directly involved with the investment management function of the firm. Specific areas covered within the operational function of a firm include fund accounting, trade operations, compliance, and information technology.

Comparing Investment and Operational Functions

The investment and operational functions of a fund management firm operate with both the same goal of promoting the profitability of the firm and its investments. Each function goes about accomplishing this goal in different ways. As we outlined in the previous section, the investment function is focused on allocating and investing capital. The operational function is not directly involved in these functions, but instead supports the work of the investment function. Despite its supporting role, this does not make the work of the operational function any less important. Without the operational function, the investment function could not operate.

Operations Role in Facilitating Investment Procedures

To best understand the role of operations in facilitating the investment procedures of a fund manager, let us consider a straightforward example of an alternative investment fund seeking to make an investment in a publicly traded stock. The job of the investment function in this case would be to determine initially which stock to invest in. Then the investment function will next make a series of determinations relating to the purchase of this stock. These can include the following:

- At what price, or price range, should the stock be purchased at?
- Are there any restrictions regarding the purchase—such as if all of the desired quantity cannot be purchased, then none is to be purchased (i.e. all or nothing)?
- When to purchase the stock?

As is common in practice, the stock in our example will not be the only investment the fund manager makes. Instead, it will be part of a series of investments that will be held together in a *portfolio* or *portfolio of investments*. In practice, a portfolio of investments is also referred to as a *fund*. When an investment is part of a portfolio, the specific answers to the questions above will often depend on a number of other considerations that relate not only to the specific characteristics of the particular stock. Portfolio management considerations, such as the amount of capital being managed, view about how this new investment in the stock will influence the overall larger portfolio and macroeconomic views about the larger market. After the portfolio manager has developed answers to these questions, the fund would then seek to purchase the stock.

Up until this point in the process, the operational function has not been engaged. Once the decision is made to make an investment, and the investment function has developed a set of rules or guidelines surrounding the way in which the investment is to be made (i.e. how much to invest, when and what other restrictions may be in place), then the operational function takes over to implement the investment function's instructions. The first step in this process would be for the operations function to proceed to place the trade in the requested stock via a process known as *execution*. The trading process is discussed in more detail in Chap. 2. After execution and the remainder of the trading process is complete, then the appropriate cash needs to be transferred to fund and settle the trade. The cash management process is discussed in more detail in Chap. 3. Additionally, the operations function will perform certain pre-trade and post-trade compliance checks to ensure that any specific regulatory of fund-specific compliance guidelines has not been violated. The compliance processes of the operational function are discussed in Chap. 4.

A number of third-party vendors, commonly referred to as *service providers*, may also be involved in several aspects of the trading process including facilitating the actual execution of the trade, the compliance oversight of the trade and processing the accounting for the trade after execution. The role of service providers in alternative investment fund manager operations is discussed in Chap. 5. The information technology supporting the phones, computers and relevant software need to be operational to process the trade, and follow up on post-trade procedures must also be working properly to support the entire trading process. The information technology process is discussed in Chap. 6.

Dependency of the Investment Function on the Operational Functions

There are a number of similarities between the investment and operational functions of alternative investment funds. Firstly, we have already introduced the concept that both the investment and operational functions have the same broad goal of promoting the profitability of the firm. Beyond that, the investment and operational functions share a number of other similarities. This is by design due to the fact that they are complementary functions. One cannot operate without the other, and both the investment and the operational functions need to be aware of what the other is doing in order to function effectively. In this way, the operational and investment functions are similar in that they both overlap in a number of different areas. Consider the previous trading example outlined in the previous section. Without the appropriate guidance from the investment function, the operational function would have no trade to execute, and no trading-related compliance activity to oversee.

To be clear, this relationship is not a one-way street and the investment function is not always leading the operational function. The activities of the investment function may be dependent upon the capabilities of the operational function. For example, consider the situation where the investment professionals at a fund manager have previously only traded US equity securities but based on recent changes in market conditions have now decided that they want to start trading in Korean securities. The operational function at the fund manager, however, may not be at all capable of supporting this activity. Alternatively, if the operational function might be eventually capable of supporting trading in Korean securities, they might not be set up to start doing so immediately. The reasons for this could include the following:

- The fund manager's trading systems may not be configured to interact electronically with Korean securities exchanges.
- The firm may not have in place the appropriate agreements and contracts to deal with Korean trading counterparties.
- The compliance function may not have yet had a chance to evaluate to implement procedures to comply with relevant compliance and regulatory requirements that may be in place when trading Korean securities.

In this case, therefore, the investment function would have to simply wait for the operations function to implement the appropriate protocols prior to beginning trading in Korean securities. On the other hand, if the investment function had given prior notice to the operations function that in the future they would likely want to start beginning to trade in a new market such as Korea, then the operational function could have made the appropriate preparations so that trading could commence once the investment function wanted to begin trading.

Another example of the ways in which the investment function may be dependent on the operational function would be if, instead of seeking to enter a new position, such as in the Korean securities example above, the investment function sought to gain more information about their options prior to adding to or exiting their position. One common piece of information investment professionals would wish to review in this case would be what is known as an *exposure report*. These reports can show a wide variety of information about the various exposures a fund manager may have to different areas that may be of interest to the investment professionals ultimately making a decision about how to proceed with a particular investment. If a fund manager, for example, manages several different funds, then they may wish to see what their aggregate exposure to a certain security, industry or region is across all the various funds managed, as compared the specific exposures in a single fund. In this case, the firm must have the operational capabilities to run these reports. This would require the appropriate databases and software from which to pull this data. Then the firm would need the capabilities to actually run and display this information in a readable format. Furthermore, if the investment function would like this report to be run in real time as compared to on a historical basis, then additional capabilities would be required. In this way, the operational function not only supports the investment function, but the investment function could not make a fully informed investment decision without the capabilities of the operational function.

While there is a co-dependency between operational and investment functions at an alternative investment fund manager, a number of differences also exist between these functions. A key difference is that the modern operational functions at alternative investment firms relates to the use of service providers. The investment function may engage with third-party providers on a limited basis such as to purchase third-party investment research. The modern operational function, however, is far more reliant on third-party service providers as compared to the investment function. To be clear, the work of some providers such as prime brokers and other trading counterparties consists of both investment and operational components.

What Is Unique About Alternative Investments Operations?

Alternative investment funds merit special consideration from an operational perspective. Part of the reason for this is because of the unique investment activities of alternative investment funds as compared to more traditional funds. To demonstrate this difference, let us compare what are known as traditional investments to alternative investments. *Traditional investments* are those investments that adhere to classical investment strategies and typically focus on security appreciation. A classic example of traditional investment is a type of fund known as a mutual fund. Mutual funds generally only purchase securities with the goal of profiting from the rise in the price of a security. This is typically known as going long a security or a *long-only investment strategy*. Let us now consider an alternative investment, such as a hedge fund. Depending on the hedge fund strategy employed, most hedge funds will purchase securities seeking to profit if a security goes up in value (i.e. going long the investment) in the same way a mutual fund would. Hedge funds typically also are nimbler than mutual funds and will also seek to profit if a security declines in value. This is known as *going short* or *shorting a security*. A common hedge fund strategy that employs bets on both the long and the short side of a security is known as a long-short strategy.

Now let us consider the operational aspects of the traditional versus alternative investment strategy. The long-only mutual fund only has to perform relatively straightforward operational procedures to account for the purchase, recording, valuation and ultimately selling of the security. These types of straightforward procedures are also known as *plain vanilla operations*.

In the case of the hedge fund however, several additional complexities are present. First of all, the universe of investable securities for the hedge fund is likely much larger than the mutual fund. This larger investable universe requires the hedge funds operations and accompanying operational systems to be more complex. Furthermore, by employing a more flexible trading strategy a hedge fund will likely participate in a more actual trade of securities as compared to a mutual fund. The number of trades a fund executes is commonly referred to as its *trade volume* or simply *volume*. With larger trade volume, the hedge funds operations must process more trades as compared to an alternative fund.

Another point of consideration is that the actual securities invested in by the hedge fund, may be more complex to account for from an operations perspective. For example, a hedge fund may invest in private loans with unique payment features to the holder (i.e. the hedge fund in this example). Accounting for this type of position from an operations perspective is entirely different and more complex than a straightforward position such as equity in a public company.

Continuing this example, a nonpublicly traded security, such as a private loan position, is not as easily valued as a long-only equity position. In this case, the hedge fund must follow a more complex series of procedures than simply looking up the price of an equity position from a data feed. The private loan position does not have a public market and, therefore, will have what is known as less liquidity. For less liquid positions, more resource-intensive and costly procedures must be employed such as security, or what are known as valuation quotes from brokers. These are known as broker-quoted positions. Alternatively, specialized third-party valuation agents may be hired to assist in calculating valuations or the fund manager may directly price the position themselves. This is known as a manager marked position. In either case, the procedure is more complex for these less liquid positions.

Another complexity of alternative investments, such as hedge funds, as compared to long-only funds, is that they typically tend to trade in a broader investible universe not only from a securities perspective, but also from a geographic perspective. When a fund manager trades in multiple markets, the complexity of the operational procedures supporting that investment activity is also increased. In many cases, an alternative investment manager would need to establish new relationships with service providers that service the markets across the globe where it is trading. Additionally, different countries have different compliance and regulatory rules that must be adhered to when investing in those markets. Finally, not all investment may be made in the same currency. In these cases, the alternative investment managers operational procedures must be equipped to address foreign exchange rate calculations and holding multicurrency-denominated positions.

Different Alternative Investment Strategies Merit Specific Operational Practices

In the previous section, we outlined the reasons why alternative investment operations are unique and require special consideration as compared to traditional managers. Within the universe of alternative investments itself, different alternative investment strategies may require further operations customization and refinement to best address their specific investment activities. We have already discussed some of the unique requirements of hedge funds. In Chaps. 8 and 9, we will discuss specifics related to two other alternative investment strategies known as private equity and hedge funds, respectively. As compared to a hedge fund, private equity funds typically invest directly into private securities such as taking ownership in shares of a start-up company. The operations procedures related to the processing of investments in private equity are different than accounting for securities that trade more frequently. To be clear, this is different than considerations of whether the securities are publicly traded or illiquid.

It should also be noted that despite the fact that there are traditional investible universes for hedge funds and private equity, today in many cases a hedge fund may hold positions in a less-liquid private equity–like positions. A hedge fund that makes these types of investments may be referred to as a *hybrid hedge fund* or a *hybrid fund*. Similarly, a private equity fund may in select circumstances make limited investments in hedge fund–like positions. In either case, the operational issues related to the specific securities held are the same. The additional complexity in hybrid funds comes from the fact that they are now holding positions of the types commonly held by both hedge funds and private equity funds.

Operational Risk Management: Trading Operations and Compliance Example

The proper management of operations at an alternative investment fund is focused not only on generating process efficiency but also on preventing violations of internal policies and procedures as well as laws and regulations. One example of an operational area that is full of these types of considerations is trading operations. From an operational perspective, the trading process involves a number of risks. These risks can relate to the actual operational processes supporting the trading process but can also relate to other areas such as compliance. One of the common compliance risks related to trading is called *front running*. Front running is a process whereby trading occurs ahead of client trades. Under common front running schemes, a trader will have information that the fund for which they work will intend to utilize a certain trade implementation strategy.

Prior to entering into the trade for the fund for which they work, the trader will then enter into trades for their own account first in anticipation of the profits that will ensue based on the much larger trading activity of the funds. In this way, the trader is effectively disadvantaging the full benefit of the trading activity of the fund for their own benefit. An example of a regulatory action against related to front running activity was in 2013 when the SEC charged a Dallas, Texas, -based senior equity trader at Cushing ML Asset Management with secretly executing hundreds of trades through his wife's accounts.[2] Another example occurred in 2011, when the United Kingdom's Financial Conduct Authority (FCA) fined a firm known as Swift Trade for £8,000,000 for activity related to trade layering allegations:[3]

A second common trading compliance risk is known as layering. In order to discuss layering, it is useful to understand some additional trading terminology first. When certain compliance violations occur in situations such as layering, they relate to a concept known as *non-economic trading*. Non-economic trading is when a fund enters into trading without which there is an economic rationale to do so. Non-economic trading is commonly utilized in market manipulation schemes such as layering. One tool commonly utilized in non-economic trading schemes is a *matched order*. The US Securities and Exchange Commission (SEC) defines a matched order as, "a coordinated order for the purchase or sale of a security—that is, an order placed with the knowledge that another order (or orders) of substantially the same size, at substantially the same time, and at substantially the same price, has been or will be entered."[4] Related to matched orders is something known as a *wash trade.* The SEC defines a wash trade as one for which there is no change in beneficial ownership.[5] The term "beneficial ownership" has special meaning in a regulatory context under SEC rules, but a beneficial owner includes any person who maintains the power to sell a security they own.[6] When there is a wash trading scheme where no change in beneficial ownership occurs, it means the trader, or the fund for which they are trading, is entering into trades with other entities that they effectively control. In essence you are trading with different legal versions of yourself under a wash trade scheme for the purposes of market manipulations.

Layering refers to a strategy that may be employed by a hedge fund utilizing an investment strategy known as *high-frequency trading* or *HFT*. Specifically, layering is where a high-frequency trading hedge fund places and then cancels orders under a matched order scheme. When doing this the hedge fund never intended to make the purchase to begin with, and merely entered the trades in order to manipulate (i.e. inflate or deflate) security prices. An example of a regulatory action against a fund related to layering activity occurred in 2011, when the United Kingdom's Financial Conduct Authority (FCA) fined a firm known as Swift Trade for £8,000,000. The FCA final decision notice summarized the trade layering activity by Swift Trade undertaken as follows:[7]

2.1—The FSA has decided to take this action as a result of the behavior of Swift Trade during the period 1 January 2007 to 4 January 2008 ("the Relevant Period"). Throughout the Relevant Period, Swift Trade systematically and deliberately engaged in a form of manipulative trading activity known as "layering". This manipulative trading caused a succession of small price movements in a wide range of individual shares on the London Stock Exchange ("the LSE") throughout the Relevant Period from which Swift Trade was able to profit. The trading activity involved tens of thousands of orders, was repeated on many occasions and was conducted in many different shares over the Relevant Period.

2.2—Layering involves entering relatively large orders on one side of the LSE order book ("the order book"), which has the effect of moving the share price as the market adjusts to the fact that there has been an apparent shift in the balance of supply and demand. This is then followed by a trade on the opposite side of the order book which takes advantage of, and profits from, the share price movement. This is in turn followed by a rapid deletion of the large orders which had been entered in order to cause the movement in price, and by a repetition of this behavior in reverse on the other side of the order book. Swift Trade placed the large orders in order to give a false and misleading impression of supply and demand. The large orders were not intended to be traded. They were carefully placed close enough to the touch price (i.e. the best bid and offer prevailing in the market at the time) to give a false and misleading impression of supply and demand, but far enough away to minimize the risk that they would be executed. They were deleted in seconds in order to further minimize the risk that they would be traded. The trading activity caused many individual share prices to be positioned at an artificial level, from which Swift Trade profited directly.

Swift Trade subsequently went out of business and the firm was dissolved.[8]

It should be noted that there is a related activity to layering called *spoofing*. An example of how spoofing works would be when a fund initiates a position, through either a single trade or a series of trades. The purpose of this is to create a new, and better for the trader, bid price or ask price on the security. After the trader has initiated the first spoofing position, another trade is then executed in the opposite side of the original trade(s). This second, opposite-side position ultimately results in market manipulation because the execution of this trade is at a more beneficial price than the trader would have been likely to obtain in the absence of the original order. A historical example of a regulatory action against related to spoofing can be found in a complaint filed by the US Commodity Futures Trading Commission (CFTC) on October 19, 2015, where the CFTC charged a Chicago trader and his propriety trading company with spoofing-related market manipulation activities. The CFTC press release related to this case summarized the activity in this case as follows:[9]

The U.S. Commodity Futures Trading Commission (CFTC) today filed a civil Complaint in the U.S. District Court for the Northern District of Illinois, charging Igor B. Oystacher and his proprietary trading company, 3 Red Trading LLC (3 Red), both of Chicago, Illinois, with spoofing and employment of a manipulative and deceptive device while trading futures on four different futures exchanges.

According to the CFTC Complaint, on at least 51 trading days between December 2011 and January 2014, Oystacher and 3 Red intentionally and repeatedly engaged in a manipulative and deceptive spoofing scheme while trading in at least five futures products on at least four exchanges: the E-Mini S&P 500 (S&P 500) futures contracts on the Chicago Mercantile Exchange (CME); crude oil and natural gas futures contracts on the New York Mercantile Exchange (NYMEX); copper futures contracts on the Commodity Exchange Inc. (COMEX); and the volatility index (VIX) futures contract on CBOE Futures Exchange (CFE). The Complaint explains that their scheme created the appearance of false market depth that Oystacher and 3 Red exploited to benefit their own interests, while harming other market participants.

Aitan Goelman, the CFTC's Director of Enforcement, commented: 'Spoofing seriously threatens the integrity and stability of futures markets because it discourages legitimate market participants from trading. The CFTC is committed to prosecuting this conduct and is actively cooperating with regulators around the world in this endeavor.'

The Complaint alleges that Oystacher and 3 Red engaged in this scheme by manually placing large passive orders on one side of the market at or near the best bid or offer price, which they intended to cancel before execution—and thus are regarded as "spoof orders." These orders were placed through accounts owned by 3 Red, to create the false impression of growing market interest to trade in a certain direction (to either buy or sell) and to induce other market participants into placing orders on the same side of the market and at similar price levels as the spoof orders. According to the Complaint, Oystacher and 3 Red would then cancel or attempt to cancel all of the spoof orders before they were executed and virtually simultaneously "flip" their position from buy to sell (or vice versa) by placing at least one aggressive order on the other side of the market at the same or better price to trade with market participants that had been induced to enter the market by the spoof orders that were just canceled.

This strategy allowed Oystacher and 3 Red to buy or sell futures contracts in quantities and at price levels that would not have otherwise been available to them in the market, absent the spoofing conduct, the Complaint alleges.

Ultimately the claims in this case were settled and a $2.5 million fine was paid in the case.[10]

Chapter Summary

This chapter provided an introduction to the subject of alternative investment operations. We began by defining alternative investments and providing an overview of the importance of classifying fund manager investment and operational activities. As part of this discussion,, we provided an overview of the role of operations in facilitating investment activities. We also analyzed the dependency of the investment function on the operations function. Next, we discussed several of the unique aspects of alternative investment operations. We also outlined how different alternative investment strategies merited specific operational strategies. Finally, we concluded with an example of operational risk management in trading operations. In the next chapter, we will discuss trade operations in more detail.

Notes

1. *See* Anson, Mark, "Handbook of Alternative Assets," Hoboken, September 2006.
2. Securities and Exchange Commission, SEC Charges Dallas-Based Trader With Front Running, May 24, 2013, available at: https://www.sec.gov/news/press-release/2013-2013-93htm.
3. Financial Conduct Authority, Decision Notice, May 6, 2011, available at: https://www.fca.org.uk/publication/decision-notices/swift_trade.pdf.
4. See Securities and Exchange Commission v. AutoChina International Limited et al. available at: https://www.sec.gov/litigation/complaints/2012/comp-pr2012-59.pdf.
5. *Id.*
6. Securities and Exchange Commission, Schedule 13D, available at: https://www.sec.gov/fast-answers/answerssched13htm.html.
7. Financial Conduct Authority, Decision Notice, May 6, 2011, available at: https://www.fca.org.uk/publication/decision-notices/swift_trade.pdf.
8. J. Treanor, "Investment firm Swift Trade loses appeal over £8m fine for market abuse," *The Guardian*, January 28, 2013.
9. Commodity Futures Trading Commission, Release Number 7264-15, October 19, 2015, available at: https://www.cftc.gov/PressRoom/PressReleases/pr7264-15.
10. M. Dave, "Head of 3Red Trading Settles CFTC Claims Engaged in Spoofing," *The Wall Street Journal*, December 21, 2016.

2

Trade Operations: Execution, Settlement and Reconciliation

Introduction to Trade Operations

In Chap. 1, we introduced the term "fund manager." For reference, a fund manager is a type of investment structure whereby investors give money to an individual or organization to investment on their behalf. All fund managers must then proceed to actually invest this capital. Hedge funds typically invest this capital by means of a process that is known as *trading*.

There are many forms of trading however; one of the more common examples is where a hedge fund decides to put investment capital to work by making an investment in a publicly traded security. In this case, there are a number of specific steps that must be followed from both an investment and an operational perspective to actually enact this trade and transfer ownership of the security to the hedge fund. In this chapter, we will focus on understanding the operational tasks involved in this process.

What Is Being Traded

Hedge fund trades in many other types of securities in addition to public equities. It should be noted that in practice the term "security" is also sometimes referred to as an *instrument* or *trading instrument*. These securities can include:

- Equities
- Commodities

© The Author(s) 2020
J. Scharfman, *Alternative Investment Operations*,
https://doi.org/10.1007/978-3-030-46629-9_2

- Debt securities such as bonds and private credit
- Currencies

However, other types of trades could involve what are known as *derivatives*. A "derivative" is a general term for a type of bilateral contract between two parties. Within the broader class of derivatives, hedge funds typically trade in *options*. Options are a specific type of derivative contracts between two different parties. In an option contract one party is not directly purchasing ownership in something, but instead is purchasing a right to buy or sell a security at a specific price within a certain period of time.

One common form of option is a call option, sometimes just called a call. When a buyer purchases a call, they have the right to purchase a security at a specific price at some point in the future. It should be noted that in the case of a *call option* the buyer has a right to do something, but they are not required to do so. If they do nothing, the option will simply expire. Another common form of an option is a *put option*, or simply a put. A put gives the buyer the right to sell securities at a predetermined price on or before the expiration of the option. Options can be utilized in different ways either in conjunction with underlying security holdings or through combinations of different types of options to create what are known as *option trading strategies*.

Hedge funds typically utilize options trading strategies to control or hedge portfolio risk. They are also utilized to facilitate specific bets on specific investment outcomes

Trade Idea Generation

Prior to entering into a trade, regardless of what the substance of the actual trade is, a hedge fund must decide what it would actually like to trade. In many cases, hedge funds may focus their investment activities around a particular *investment theme* or *style*. An example of an investment style would be a hedge fund that is focused on investing a specific regional market such as Asian equities or, more specifically, Chinese equities. An investment style may also be centered around a particular marketplace such as a hedge fund that investment globally technology stocks. Additionally, a hedge fund's investment theme could be driven by size such as focusing on small to mid-capitalization. In practice each of these areas, as well as others, could be combined to create a unique style for different hedge funds.

Using the global technology fund as an example, we can next turn to the process by which the fund would determine which technology stocks to invest in. While the specifics on underlying equity analysis are best left to other books, our focus here is on the process that is followed as opposed to the actual analysis that is conducted. While the specific process employed may vary from fund to fund, it usually begins with an individual known as a *research analyst* forming an opinion about a particular potential investment opportunity. Continuing our example, let us assume that the research analyst decides that she believes the prices of Google stock will increase by $5 within the next two months.

Once the opportunity is identified, the research analyst would then likely produce a document known as an *investment memorandum*, which would summarize this opinion and provide appropriate support. The next likely step in the process would be for the investment memorandum to be circulated throughout the hedge fund to the research analysts other investment colleagues. The investment colleagues would then likely discuss the memorandum informally and in more formal meetings.

At many hedge funds, a weekly investment meeting is held where both the existing holdings in a hedge funds portfolio and any potential new investment opportunities are discussed. In our example, the investment memorandum, or a revised version of it, would be discussed at the weekly investment meeting. At this meeting, the research analyst would likely be asked to walkthrough her investment thesis as to the reasons for the anticipated price risk in google stock, and then answer a series of questions. After the investment memorandum was discussed, a decision as to next steps would likely be reached. One option would be for a group of individuals known as an *investment committee* to make a determination as to whether or not proceed with implementing an investment strategy based on the research analysts investment thesis on Google.

A hedge fund's investment committee typically consists of a group of senior investment professionals at the fund and is typically chaired by the firm's chief investment officer (CIO). Depending on the size and structure of the hedge fund organization, the decision of the investment committee may commonly be required to be made either unanimously or by majority decision. It is important to note that the investment committee does not only vote to approve investment activities that result in new purchases for the hedge fund but may also take action on adding to existing positions, trimming or selling out of positions in the hedge fund's portfolio as well.

Trading Strategy Compared to Trade Idea Generation

The investment thesis of the research analyst in our example was that Google stock will increase by $5 within the next two months; the question of actually how to implement this is a different matter. An *investment thesis* in this way can be thought of as a general idea or hypothesis about actions that will happen in a particular market or to a specific security. The way a hedge fund actually makes money from an investment thesis is a different matter entirely. This is where the concept of a trading strategy comes in. A *trading strategy* is the way in which a hedge fund actually implements an investment thesis in the markets. To understand a hedge fund's trading strategy, we must first understand the *investment style* of the fund. Investment style can also be referred to as the *investment strategy* of a fund.

Investment style refers to the general approach taken by a fund toward generating *alpha*.

Alpha can also be represented by the Greek letter α. Without delving too deeply into the technical aspects of its definition, alpha refers to profit. It can be compared broadly to another concept *beta*. Beta can be represented by the Greek letter β. Once again without become overly technical, on a high-level beta can be thought of as volatility in the form of market risk. This type of risk is also referred to as undiversifiable risk or market risk.

The most common hedge fund strategies include the following:

- Equity long / short—An investment strategy based around the combination of long and short equity positions as well as potential options and futures.
- Global macro—An investment strategy that focuses on a global macroeconomic approach toward investing.
- Short selling (or short-biased)—This investment strategy involves and maintains a net short exposure and seeks to profit from a declining market or declines in a particular security.
- Arbitrage strategies—These include a variety of arbitrage approaches including convertible bond arbitrage, relative value arbitrage and fixed income arbitrage. It should be noted that the term *arbitrage* technically means a riskless profit. Somewhat counterintuitively, even though these investment strategies have the term "arbitrage" in their title, they are not riskless.

- Event driven—This is a transaction-focused investment strategy that focuses on profit generation in situations such as corporate bankruptcies and mergers and acquisitions. One type of event-driven strategy is known as merger arbitrage, which can focus investing around situations relating to mergers and acquisitions as well as distressed companies.
- Market neutral—This investment strategy maintains long and short exposure in an attempt to eliminate their overall market exposure and focus exclusively, therefore, on security selection.
- Credit—This investment strategy focuses on trading in credit and debt securities such as mortgage-backed securities (MBS) and collateralized loan obligations (CLOs).

Returning to our previous example, if the investment thesis is that the price of Google is going to increase by $5 in the next two months and our manager follows an equity long / short investment strategy to actually trade this thesis, the trading strategy might be to purchase Google stock (i.e. go long Google) and short a stock with negative correlation to Google; for our purposes, we will make up a company called Company X. Now that we have our investment thesis and general trading strategy, the next step in the trading process is for the trade to actually be put into place. This process is called trade implementation. *Trade implementation* is the execution of a trading strategy.

Trade Implementation

In its most simple instance, continuing our Google investment thesis, a hedge fund would decide that it wants to take a long position in Google and then goes out to the stock market and buys Google. There are several questions the hedge fund has to answer before it actually proceeds with trade implementation. Firstly, how many of these shares do they wish to purchase? Is it $100 worth, $10 million worth, or some other amount? Another question to consider is, when does the fund want to purchase the shares? It should be noted that the process of purchasing a position for the first time in a portfolio, either long or short, is known as *initiating a position*.

The hedge fund should also consider if the fund wants to purchase an entire fixed amount of Google stock all at once, or, instead, does it want to spread out the purchases of this position over several trades? Most large investment managers, such as hedge funds, usually purchase stocks in large quantities through what are known as *block trades*. A block trade typically involves at least 10,000 shares of a stock, but in practice hedge funds can institute block trades well in excess of those figures. Block trades also do not need to be executed in the public markets, and in practice many block trades are negotiated between funds and large institutions in private.

When considering the best trading strategy to implement, a hedge fund must consider the impact the trade will have on a market. For example, consider a penny stock that has relatively low liquidity and then all of a sudden a hedge fund makes a large block trade in that stock. This increase in unusual trading activity would likely cause higher demand for the stock among market participants and the price of the stock would go up. The hedge fund may not want to send a signal to the markets in such a direct way and, therefore, will engage in other trading techniques. One approach is to break up a large block into smaller blocks, thereby reducing the amount of activity in each trade. Additionally, spacing out the smaller blocks will also lessen the market impact.

Another technique a fund may use to lessen the market impact of a block trade is to work with an intermediary to assist in performing the trade. In practice, many hedge funds utilize the block trading services of entities known as *broker-dealers*. A broker-dealer can be an individual or more likely a firm that buyer buys or sells securities on behalf of its clients. Many of the broker-dealers that hedge funds work with are large investment banks. The investment bank, acting as the broker-dealer, would serve as the intermediary in the transaction between the hedge fund and another party on the other side of the trade.

Order Entry

Pre-Trade Blotters

The trade implementation process begins with a procedure known as *order entry*. Order entry is when personnel at a hedge fund first begin the process of logging the trading instructions. Specifically, order entry involves the details of the specific trade being loaded into a computer system. In some cases, a fund manager maintains a system that they utilize to first load the specific desired details of a trade into. The system used by the manager is generally one of two types. The first type is one that the manager may have developed internally themselves; this is known as a *proprietary system*.

When trades are first entered into the trading system, they are usually first loaded onto what is known as a *pre-trade blotter*. A pre-trade blotter is a document that is utilized to record the intended details of each trade before they are entered into.

Electronic Versus Physical Pre-Trade Blotters

Historically, trade blotters were physical paper documents where trading details were recorded. Today, the use of paper-based trading blotters is virtually unheard of and electronic pre-trade blotters are utilized. Some hedge funds log pre-trade information on electronic spreadsheets via programs such as Microsoft Excel. Other funds utilized more sophisticated traded systems to log the bulk of their trading information. These systems are called *order management systems*, often abbreviated simply as *OMS*.

An example of a spreadsheet-based pre-trade blotter is included in Table 2.1.

Pre-Trade Compliance Checks

After a trade has been logged on the pre-trade blotter, either via a spreadsheet or in the fund's order management system, the next step is to typically perform a number of checks on the actual trade. The goal of these checks is to ensure that if the trade were to proceed to actually being executed by the fund, it would not violate any compliance rules. Today, the bulk of these *pre-trade compliance checks* are automatically performed in the order management system via a series of *compliance trading rules* that are coded into the trading system.

There are two general categories of compliance trading rules. The first category referred to as *mandatory compliance rules* because if the rule is applicable to the fund, it has no choice but to comply with it. In general, mandatory compliance rules come from two primary sources. The first source is from legislation. Specifically, laws affecting the ways fund managers trade may be developed by legislative bodies such as the US Congress and the UK Parliament. The second primary source of mandatory compliance rules come from financial regulators. It should be noted that as a result of the influence of regulators on mandatory compliance, mandatory compliance is also sometimes referred to as *regulatory compliance*. The rules are promulgated by external regulators such as the US Securities and Exchange Commission (SEC), Commodity and Futures Trading Commission (CFTC), the National Futures Association (NFA) and the UK Financial Conduct Authority (FCA).

At any point in time, regulators have a series of trading rules and guidelines on file that covered funds must follow where applicable. These rules are not set in stone and may be subject to revision either via an adjustment to existing rules or brand new rules. Commonly, the regulators do not just implement these rules out of the blue but instead go through a proposal and feedback

Table 2.1 Example Spreadsheet Pre-Trade Blotter

Ticker	Trade logged by	Date	Purchase or sale	Security type	Proposed price	Shares	Proposed total trade value	Currency
TGT	Bill Smith	2/27/20	Purchase	Stock	$110	25,000	$2,750,000	USD
WMT	Tom Smith	2/27/20	Purchase	Stock	$125	26,500	$3,312,500	USD
MSI	Bill Smith	2/28/20	Purchase	Stock	$168	12,000	$2,016,000	USD
BYND	Brian Smith	2/28/20	Sale	Stock	$109	60,000	$6,540,000	USD
APRN	Bill Smith	2/28/20	Sale	Stock	$1.52	45,000	$68,400	USD
UBER	Mark Smith	2/28/20	Purchase	Stock	$35	14,000	$490,000	USD
ACB	Bill Smith	2/29/20	Sale	Stock	$1.09	17,800	$19,402	USD
TLRY	Tom Smith	2/29/20	Purchase	Stock	$1.45	30,200	$43,790	USD
CGC	Bill Smith	2/29/20	Purchase	Stock	$16	19,000	$304,000	USD
WCG	Bill Smith	2/29/20	Purchase	Stock	$352	18,500	$6,512,000	USD

period before coming to a determination as to the implementation of the final trading rule. An example of this was in January 2020 when the CFTC proposed the so-called speculative position limits on over 20 different commodities including crude oil, sugar and gold. The specific limit proposed commodities position limits of up to 25% of the deliverable supply of each commodity.[1]

The second type of compliance rules are self-imposed on funds by themselves. The fund may institute these rules based on regulatory guidance, but the point is that the fund does not have to follow them; instead, they are placing the obligation on themselves to follow the rule they have created for themselves. These are referred to as *voluntary compliance rules.*

One item that is commonly checked through the use of compliance trading rules is something that is known as *position limits.* Position limits may be implemented by regulators. An example of this is the proposed 25% CFTC limit discussed above. Position limits may also be self-imposed on funds by themselves. These self-imposed limited are examples of voluntary compliance rules. Position limits refer to the maximum amount of a specific thing that can be present in a portfolio or group of portfolios. For example, a hedge fund may institute a rule that states that no more than 5% of a portfolio can be in the share of a single company. Another common variation on position limit rules may be that a portfolio cannot have more than 10% of its holdings in securities from a particular country or region. Some organizations for ethical reasons also institute bans on investing in certain types of industries such as tobacco or firearms; these too are position limits in that the acceptable limit is 0% and any portfolio exposure to these industries is unacceptable in this scenario.

An example of the way a compliance rule such as position limits would be implemented in an order management system on a pre-trade basis would be first for the trade to be entered into the pre-trade blotter. Next, prior to proceeding to the next stage in the trading processes, the OMS compares the existing holdings of the portfolio on a pre-trade basis to the portfolio holdings if the trade had hypothetically been executed. If on a post-trade basis the new portfolio would have violated position limits, then the potential trade has failed the pre-trade compliance check.

If a pre-trade compliance check shows that the potential trade would have indeed violated a compliance rule, then both the trader and the hedge fund's compliance department would typically receive a notification of the potential compliance rule violation. This is commonly known as a *red flag notification*. It would then be up to the firm to investigate the potential trade and determine if they would like to completely scrap the potential trade entirely or modify it so that it can be executed in line with the compliance trading rules. In general, when a red flag notification is triggered by an order management system, the OMS will not allow the trade to proceed. This is known as a *hard coded compliance rule*.

While red flag notifications do occur, in practice many portfolio managers and traders keep a close eye on the composition of their portfolio and are familiar with general compliance rules relating to their funds. Therefore, they commonly will have a good idea as to whether a proposed trade would likely violate a compliance trading rule. The more common compliance trading rule notification as a result of pre-trade compliance checks is something known as a *yellow flag notification*. Yellow flag notifications are generated by an order management system when a compliance rule would not actually be violated by it would come close to be violated.

Some compliance rules do not lend themselves to yellow flag notifications. An example of this would be a total prohibition on trading in tobacco stocks in a portfolio. There is no gray area with regards to this rule. Either the fund follows the rule or it violates it. Other rules, such as position limits, better lend themselves to yellow flag analysis. For example, consider a fund that maintains a 10% position limit on trading in any single company. Further, assume that the current position of a portfolio in the stock of a hypothetical company, Company X, is 6%. If a trader was considering a trade that would boost the existing holdings from 6% to 9%, would this be a violation of the 10% limit? No; however, many funds would like to know that they are getting close to the 10% limit so that they can more closely monitor positions. One reason for this is that the value and, therefore, the size of position in the portfolio are in flux over time based on market activities. If a position is at 9% of the portfolio and the stock of Company X appreciates suddenly, it could easily become in excess of 10% of the portfolio. Therefore, it is useful for the fund to have a notification when compliance trading rules such as position limits are being approached. In these cases, the fund can set up a yellow flag notification to provide an alert when position limits are close to being breached. The fund can set the desired yellow flag notifications at whatever levels they chose. Yellow flag notifications are similar to a compliance concept known as a *near-miss register* in which a fund will note activities that are across the firm, not just necessarily related to trading activities, and that are not actual violations of compliance activities but are approaching violations.

Other types of pre-trade compliance trading rule relate to potential trades in securities which the fund may not be able to execute trades in due to reasons other than portfolio limits. One example of this relates to a concept known as *material non-public information*, also referred to by the abbreviation *MNPI*. MNPI is also referred to as *insider information*. While there are very technical definitions of MNPI, in summary it can be thought of as information which a fund has gained access to, that if it were to trade on, it would significantly influence the market value of a security (i.e. material) and which has not been made available in a public forum (i.e. non-public). Utilizing MNPI to trade is illegal in the United States and most other jurisdictions. In recent years, there have been a number of inquiries related to hedge fund manager's use of expert networks and trading on insider information. To prevent trading on MNPI, many funds will keep a list of any securities from which they may have learned about MNPI. This is commonly referred to as a *watch list* or a *restricted list*. A fund will typically hard code the names of securities on the restricted list into the order management system. When a trader enters a potential trade, the OMS would then perform a comparison of the potential trade against the restricted list. If the securities in the potential trade are on the restricted list, then a red flag alert would be triggered, and the trade could not proceed.

Trade Execution

After a trade has been entered into the pre-trade blotter, and the pre-trade compliance checks have then been completed in the order management system, the next step is to proceed to actually completing the trade with someone else. This is a process known as *trade execution*.

The other party involved on the other side of a trade is referred to as a *trading counterparty* or, simply, *counterparty*. For example, if a hedge fund is buying 500 shares of Google stock, then the entity selling the hedge fund the Google stock would be its trading counterparty. As with most of the modern trading processes, many funds execute trades electronically. In some cases, especially for markets in securities with less liquidity, trade execution may take place over the phone. For reference, before the advent of electronic trading systems, historically many funds utilized phone-based trading systems.

The trade execution process can vary depending on the types of securities being traded. A common type of security is one that is known as an *exchange traded security*. This simply means that the security, such as Google stock, is traded on an exchange such as the New York Stock Exchange (NYSE). Other types of securities are not traded on an exchange, but instead primarily are traded in a format known as *over-the-counter (OTC)* through *brokers*.

When a fund trades through a broker, they may contact a single broker directly to assist in making a trade. Alternatively, a fund may reach out to several brokers to make it known that they are interested in trading a particular security and see which brokers respond and what potential prices they are providing for the trade. These responses from brokers are commonly referred to as an *indication of interest*. Once the fund selects which broker, or brokers with which it would like to execute the trade, the broker will then proceed in executing the trade with the respective counterparties. After the trade is completed, the broker will then notify the fund trader that the trade has been executed. This notification may come via another phone call initially but is typically followed by some form of communication in writing summarizing the important details of a trade. This written notification is referred to as a *notice of execution* and may be communicated through methods such as via email or instant message.

Throughout the trading process, there are different types of brokers that a fund manager may work with. One type is known as an *executing broker*. Executing brokers are an intermediary that sit between the fund manager and the trading counterparty. Specifically, after the fund decides to execute a trade, they typically transmit the order to an executing broker first. The executing broker then communicates with trading counterparties to find the most favorable price it can for the hedge fund. This most favorable price is what is commonly known as *best execution.*

The specific steps taken by the executing broker to execute a trade largely depend on the type of security being traded by the fund. If the stock is traded via an exchange, then the executing broker may send the fund's potential order directly to the exchange. Alternatively, the executing broker may turn the order over to what is known as a *third market maker.* A market maker is a company that must regularly purchases and sells an individual security on an ongoing basis at publicly quoted prices. Market makers can participate in over-the-counter (OTC) markets. In general, OTC stocks may have more than one market maker. They can also participate in exchange traded stocks via exchanges such as the New York Stock Exchange (NYSE). Market makers for exchange traded securities are referred to as third market makers.

Another option is for an executing broker to execute trades through what is known as an *electronic communication network,* also abbreviated as an *ECN.* ECNs are generally utilized for specific types of orders called limit orders. A *limit order* is an order to buy or sell a stock at a specific price. Limit orders may not be filled if the security in question does not reach the price specified in the original limit order. This can be contrasted with a *market order* which is a buy or sell order that is to be made at the current market price. Executing brokers also may maintain their own in-house inventory of stock. As another option to fill the fund's order, an executing broker may also seek to fulfill the fund's order from its own inventory.

Executing brokers are often necessary for fund managers because they facilitate navigating large fund trades and often in a more expedient manner than if the hedge fund tried to locate the counterparty themselves. Executing brokers typically earn a commission on what is known as the bid-ask spread. A *bid price* is the highest price a buyer will pay for a security. A bid price can also be referred to as simply a "bid." Conversely, an *ask price,* also called an offer price, is the lower price a seller will sell a security for. An ask price or offer price can also be referred to as the "ask" or "offer." The difference between the bid and ask prices is known as the *spread.* Many executing brokers are also part of larger organizations known as *prime brokers.* Prime brokers provide a number of different services to fund managers including custody, financing, client services and operations support. For reference, more information on prime brokers is discussed in Chap. 5.

Trade Give-Ups

Historically, there was a framework for trading known as a *give-up*. The purpose of a give-up agreement was for a hedge fund's prime broker to consolidate the hedge fund's trading activity so that the hedge fund deals directly with a single counterparty (i.e. the prime broker) as opposed to a large number of different trading counterparties. The reason the transaction is called a give-up is because the hedge fund effectively gives up the trade between itself and the executing brokers to the prime broker. In this way, the trade is not taking place between the prime broker and executing brokers as opposed to between the hedge fund and the executing broker. The prime broker in this case is also sometimes referred to as the *give-up bank* or *spoke bank*, and the hedge fund would be referred to as the *give-up client*. This relationship also potentially allows the hedge funds to have access to increased liquidity because they are able to deal with multiple counterparties more easily as opposed to a single counterparty. The consolidation process also allows the hedge fund to reconcile trades and verify documentation with only the prime broker as opposed to a wide variety of parties. Give-up agreements can be used for a variety of instruments including over-the-counter (OTC) derivatives and equities.

Under a give-up, a hedge fund could enter into an OTC derivative trade with a variety of different counterparties. At the end of a trading session, the hedge fund's prime broker would then have transitioned the hedge fund's trade in-house and, therefore, consolidate the trade so that the hedge fund only has to deal with the prime broker as opposed to all the other trading counterparties. This process involves the prime broker to develop a series of arrangements with each different banking counterparty utilizing by the hedge fund in executing the OTC trades.[2] Another benefit of give-up agreements was that the hedge fund only had to post collateral with a single counterparty (i.e. the prime broker) and not with each multiple counterparty.

When the prime broker participated in this agreement, they also took on additional counterparty risk from the multiple counterparties that otherwise would have been directly on the books of the hedge funds. As prime brokerages became increasingly concerned about their counterparty exposures, they increasingly sought to scale back on give-up agreements. Additionally, give-back agreements in many cases were losses leading with the intention of bringing in additional business from hedge funds in other areas; however, as this business became less profitable, increasingly prime brokers transitioned away from this business.

Trade Confirmation

After a trade has been executed, the next step is a process known as *trade confirmation*. Under this process, a fund receives confirmation that the trade was actually indeed executed. As noted above, trade conformation can come in a variety of formats including phone calls, instant messages or email. These confirmations summarize the important details of a trade such as the price at which the trade was executed, the quantity of shares purchased and the time the trade was executed.

Although extremely rare today, historically some funds would have used a physical paper process. The way it would have worked would be that a fund utilized the pre-trade blotter to then generate a separate physical piece of paper known as a *trading ticket*. A human trader would have then likely executed the trade over the phone with a counterparty. After execution occurred the trader would then write down the relevant trade details on the physical trade ticket.

Once the information was on this ticket, the trader would then take the physical trading ticket over to a machine where the trade ticket would be inserted and time stamped. This trade ticket would then be given to the operations team at the fund responsible for overseeing the trade confirmation and settlement processes. While such processes have largely been phased out for more efficient, and secure, electronic processes, it is useful to put the trading process in historical context to understand how it performed prior to the use of modern computers and electronic trading.

Trade Clearing

Trade clearing is the step in the trading process where the accounts of the fund and counterparties are updated to arrange for the upcoming exchange of money for securities. In many instances, an intermediary such as a specialized clearing corporation or prime broker will step in to serve as an intermediary and reconcile orders between the parties to a trade.

Many exchanges such as the New York Stock Exchange and NASDAQ maintain specialized clearing corporations that act as an intermediary to ensure that the parties will have enough money in their accounts to complete a trade and that the trade will be completed in an efficient manner.

For funds that trade futures, a specialized entity known as a *clearing house* effectively sits between the two parties to the trade to act as a placeholder counterparty for both entities. This clearing house entity then works with both parties to the trade to ensure that all the trade details are in order and that the appropriate funds and securities are indeed in place to complete the trade. The use of a clearing house in this way is sometimes referred to as *central clearing*, because all trades are centralized through the clearing house. This can be contrasted with *bilateral clearing*, where the individual counterparties to the trade sort out to trade clearing details directly among themselves. It should be noted that the use of a clearing house does not completely remove counterparty risk from the transaction. If one side to a trade should become insolvent, the clearing house would step in to honor the trade; however, there is a possibility that the clearing house itself could fail. While this is extremely rare, there have been historical instances of clearing house failures such as the following[3]:

- The French Caisse de Liquidation in 1974—caused by unmet margin calls after a drop in sugar prices
- The Kuala Lumpur Commodities Clearing House in 1983—a result of unmet margin calls after a sharp crash in palm oil futures
- The Hong Kong Futures Exchange in 1987—the exchange closed for four days due to panic relating to unmet margin calls an equity future. The exchange was subsequently bailed out by the government.

In other cases, there have been near misses where clearing exchanges almost failed. An example of this was during the 1987 stock market crash where entities such as the Chicago Mercantile Exchange (CME), Chicago Board of Options (CBOE) and the Options Clearing Corporation (OCC) experienced difficulties related to margin calls and required bailouts to stay afloat. Another more recent almost failure of a clearing house occurred in 1999 and involved a Brazilian stock exchange known as the Bolsa de Valores, Mercadorias & Futuros de Sao Paulo. At the time, an almost 50% decline in the Brazilian Real with respect to the US dollar occurred, which led to the default of two bank clearing parties and unmet margin.[4] Ultimately, the failure of the stock exchange was prevented by a bailout by the central bank.

It is also worth noting that there have been instances where a clearing house may not be become insolvent but instead may not have been operating as it should. An example of this was in September 2019 when the US SEC and the CFTC charged the OCC with failing to establish and maintain adequate risk management policies.[5] The OCC is the only registered clearing agency for exchange listed option contracts in the US. The SEC complaint in this case outlined charges against the OCC as follows[6]:

Specifically, OCC failed to establish, implement, maintain and enforce policies and procedures reasonably designed to:

a. review its risk-based margin models and the parameters for those models on a monthly basis;
b. consider and produce margin levels commensurate with the risks and particular attributes of each relevant product cleared by OCC;
c. effectively measure, monitor, and manage its credit exposure and liquidity risk;
d. maintain a comprehensive risk management framework;
e. protect the security of certain of its information systems; and
f. provide for a well-founded, clear, transparent and enforceable legal framework for every aspect of its activities.

Ultimately, the OCC agreed to pay a combined $20 million penalty in the case that was broken out as $15 million under the SEC's order and $5 million under the CFTC's order. Additionally, the OCC agreed to hire an independent compliance auditor monitor its ongoing compliance efforts.

Historically, payments were made with physical checks and physical security certificates, but today the role of many clearing houses takes place electronically through *an automated clearing house system*. This system is also simply abbreviated as an *ACH*. Under an ACH system, when the funds are actually transferred, it is typically referred to as an *electronic funds transfer* or *EFT*.

Trade Settlement

Trade settlement refers to the step in the trading process where the exchange of money and securities between the fund and trading counterparties occurs. The specific date that this exchange occurs is referred to as the *settlement date*. The settlement date can be contrasted with the date the actual trade is executed, that is referred to as the *trade date*. Settlement for the bulk of securities is performed electronically today. Equity trades are usually settled within three business days of the trade date. A common convention for writing this framework in practice is T+3, where, "T" refers to the trade date. Government securities typically settle on T+1. The use of electronic methods of clearing and funds transfer has served to continually reduce the time period between the trade date and the settlement date. Historically, when paper checks and security certificates were utilized, there was a much larger gap between the settlement date and the trade date.

Trade Reconciliation

Trade reconciliation is the process by which the internal details of trades on the books of the fund are compared to the details of the trade with the counterparties. You may recall from our discussion above that the fund initially logged its desired trade on a pre-trade blotter during the order entry process. Then after the trade was executed, during the trade confirmation process, the fund received details from counterparties that indeed executed with summary of the important details of a trade. The reconciliation process can be thought of as another check to ensure that the details communicated among the counterparties do indeed match. A key difference is that the timing of the reconciliation process occurs after the settlement process, whereas the other checks were before the settlement. Sometimes during the settlement process the details of a trade can change slightly, which is one reasons the trade reconciliation process is important. Even if no changes occur from the settlement process, it is essential that the fund ensures that the trading records of it are maintained as well as its counterparties are accurate. If they are not, then there could be a number of adverse consequences.

An extreme example of how a trade reconciliation problem could create larger issues would be if, for example, a fund recorded incorrectly the actual name of the security purchased. For example, consider if a fund intended to execute a trade in the stock of Google's GOOGL and logged the trade in their order management system as such. However, in our example the counterparty makes a mistake and executes a trade in a different version of Google stock, GOOG. In this case, if the error is not caught during the reconciliation process, then the fund would view its portfolio as having the wrong stock. This could impact the fund in a number of different ways including fund valuations, risk management and investment management. It is likely that this error would eventually be caught either during an audit or during a review by a service provider known as a *fund administrator*; however, there would be a delay between when the trade was actually executed and when the error was caught and the problems associated with the error could compound in the interim period.

There are different kinds of reconciliation processes. The simplest version is called a *two-way reconciliation*. In this two-way framework, a fund's trading records are compared with the prime broker's records. To be clear, the prime broker is consolidating the records to the other trading counterparties that may have been utilized. Therefore, while there are two parties involved in a two-way reconciliation (i.e. the fund and the prime broker), there could actually be more parties if the prime broker executed the trade with other counterparties. Historically, reconciliations were performed manually by comparing physical paper records. Today it is commonplace for fund managers to utilize an *automated reconciliation process*. Under this automated process, a software program automatically compares the trade details from the fund's own order management system to the trading records of the prime broker. To be clear, the fund typically downloads a trading record from the prime broker on a nightly basis and uses this file to facilitate the automated reconciliation process.

Another type of reconciliation process is known as a *three-way reconciliation*. This type of reconciliation is also referred to as a *triangular reconciliation*. Under this three-way framework, a reconciliation is performed between three parties. The first two parties are the same as under a two-way reconciliation, namely the fund and prime broker counterparties. The additional party to a three-way reconciliation is the fund administrator. The administrator is a service provider that can provide a number of different services to a fund manager, one of which involves maintaining the financial *books and records* of the fund. As part of this process, the administrator also maintains a record of the fund's trading activity. Many fund administrators will have access to both the records of the fund itself, as well as receive copies of all trade confirmations for the funds. A three-way reconciliation, therefore, is more thorough than a two-way reconciliation and serves to facilitate an additional level of comparison among the various entities to a trade to ensure that both the counterparties, the fund and its service providers maintain accurate records of the trade that was actually executed and settled.

In some cases, the reconciliation process will highlight a trade that was intended to be executed but failed to execute. This is known as a *trade break*. During the reconciliation process, if there is a mismatch among the records of the fund and the counterparties or administrator as relevant, then the fund's operational personnel, in conjunction with the counterparties and administrator, will being an investigation. In some cases, the error is merely a clerical one and the records are corrected. In other cases, a more extensive investigation is required, and the funds and the counterparties may have to research their records and provide evidence to support their position to each other. This highlights another reason why the trade reconciliation process is important. In some cases, a prime broker may make a *trade error* that disadvantages the fund. These types of trade errors can result in a financial loss for the fund. In these cases, if indeed it was a genuine error on their part and the hedge fund followed the proper order submission procedures, the prime broker may be responsible to pay the fund back for the loss. The prime broker may have been unaware of the error and certainly would not be able to determine if it was indeed responsible, or the amount of the loss in question, without the appropriate documentation. In these cases, it is important for the fund to not only detect the error during the reconciliation process but also maintain appropriate records, also referred to as *trade support* to facilitate the documentation process. In other cases, the fund administrator may be the one noticing the error during the reconciliation process, and, in that case, it would work with the fund to facilitate the investigation process.

Trade Allocation

In many cases, a fund manager will implement a single investment strategy across several different funds. These different funds are sometimes referred to as *investment vehicles*, or simply *vehicles*. One primary reason for these different investment vehicles are to accommodate the needs of different investors. A common structure for hedge funds is to maintain a so-called *domestic vehicle* to accommodate investors in the country in which the hedge fund manager is domiciled. For reference, a domestic vehicle is also referred to as an onshore vehicle.

For example, a US-based hedge fund manager, whose headquarters are in New York and who is incorporated in Delaware, would likely have a Delaware-based fund as its domestic investment vehicle. This vehicle would accommodate the tax needs of most US investors.

The complement to a domestic fund is known as an *offshore vehicle*. Offshore vehicles are typically for non-US investors, or certain US investors for which the domestic fund would not be advantageous for tax purposes. One of the most common domiciles for offshore funds stemming from US managers is the Cayman Islands.

Trade allocation is the process whereby the trades of a fund completed are divided up (i.e. allocated) among a fund manager various different vehicles after they have been executed. To avoid conflicts of interest on a case-by-case basis, many funds maintain trade allocation policies that outline the procedures by which trades are to be allocated before execution, so that once they are executed the rules by which the fund will divide up the trades are clear. A common allocation procedure is known as *pro rata allocation*. Under a pro rata allocation approach, the fund manager will allocate shares in the securities purchased to different vehicles based on predetermined proportionate amounts. For example, consider a fund that purchases 100 shares of a company and each share costs a dollar for a total investment of $100 (i.e. 100 shares at a dollar each). In this case, let us further assume that the fund has a single investment strategy with domestic and offshore vehicles. If the $100 investment came entirely from the domestic or offshore vehicle, then that fund would get the shares exclusively. However, in practice this is not usually the case. Let us assume, for our example, that $60 came from the domestic fund and the remaining $40 from the offshore fund. In this case, using a pro rata allocation framework the domestic fund would therefore receive 60 shares and the offshore fund the remaining 40 shares.

While this may seem relatively straightforward, the application of a consistent trade allocation policy by a fund is important not only to the actual operational aspects of trade allocation but can also have material compliance implications. Consider, for example, that a fund maintained an onshore and an offshore vehicle, and for a variety of reasons the investment performance of the onshore fund was far superior to the offshore vehicle, despite their having materially same investment strategy. In this case, the fund manager may be presented with what they feel to be a new attractive investment opportunity to purchase shares in a new IPO at an attractive price. Continuing our example, let us also assume that the fund manager is confident this investment will be highly profitable. Although both the onshore and offshore vehicles may have capital available to purchase the pre-IPO shares, the fund manager may give more shares to the underperforming offshore vehicle. While this would boost the performance of the offshore vehicle, effectively what the fund manager is doing is benefitting the offshore investors to the detriment of the onshore investors. The process of selecting certain trade to allocate or over-allocate different funds is sometimes referred to as *cherry-picking*. This process is not equitable and also violates the compliance guidelines of many jurisdictions. Therefore, many fund managers pro rata trade allocation procedures also include guidelines regarding predetermined desired allocation size among funds so that a fund manager cannot allocate trades in a matter that is not equitable to investors across all funds it manages.

Another reason that it is important for the fund to have trade allocation procedures from an operational perspective is that a fund may manage several different investment strategies. There may be some overlap in the investment opportunity set for these different strategies, and a fund's purchase of a security would then need to be divided up among all of the appropriate investment strategies. On a related note, the fund manager may also manage a fund with its own money for internal personnel, sometimes referred to as a *proprietary capital fund* or *prop capital fund*. For these types of proprietary capital funds, trade allocation becomes a concern because investors in the firm's funds would not want the fund manager to allocate the most attractive investment opportunities to its own in-house proprietary funds as opposed to the funds it manages for external investors.

Historically, some fund managers have sought to manipulate performance through the allocation of very profitable trades, also called winning trades, among accounts after they have been executed. One historical case from 2018 involved allegations by the CFTC against an individual named Christian Robert Mayer for engaging in a fraudulent trading scheme involving unauthorized trades in cattle, crude oil and wheat futures contracts. The CFTC release on the matter summarizes the events of the case as follows[7]:

> Mayer, a registered Associated Person of a Minneapolis Commodity Trading Advisor and Introducing Broker (the IB), engaged in a fraudulent trading scheme in which he conducted unauthorized futures trading in customers' accounts, and then transferred the profitable unauthorized trades from those accounts to his personal trading account while leaving losing trades in the customers' accounts. Mayer then logged on to the online portal of the Futures Commission Merchant which carried all the accounts, accessed the transfer section of the portal, and fraudulently indicated that the reason for the trade transfer request was that he had placed the trade in the wrong account.

The CFTC Order in the case required Mr. Mayer to pay a $100,000 civil monetary penalty and imposes permanent trading and registration bans on him.

Another case from 2018, which involved allegation of cherry-picking is summarized in the following excerpt from an SEC press release[8]:

> On August 17, 2018, the Commission instituted and simultaneously settled administrative and cease-and-desist proceedings (the "Order") against Roger T. Denha ("Denha"). In the Order, the Commission found that, from at least January 2012 to November 2017, Denha, an investment adviser and investment adviser representative of BKS Advisors LLC ("BKS"), an investment adviser registered with the Commission and based in Southfield, Michigan, engaged in a fraudulent trade allocation, or "cherry-picking." Denha executed his cherry-picking scheme by unfairly allocating purchases of securities between his favored accounts (including his personal and family accounts) and his other BKS clients' accounts. Denha disproportionately allocated profitable trades to the favored accounts, and disproportionately allocated unprofitable trades to the accounts of certain advisory clients. He executed his scheme by buying the securities in an omnibus account and then waiting to allocate until after he had an opportunity to see whether the securities had increased in price.

Contemporaneously with the Order, the Commission instituted and simultaneously settled administrative and cease-and-desist against BKS (together with the Order, "Orders").

In their respective Orders, Denha was ordered to pay a total of $616,618.00 in disgorgement, prejudgment interest, and a civil money penalty and BKS was ordered to pay a $75,000.00 civil money penalty. The funds were ordered to be combined into a Fair Fund, created pursuant to Section 308(a) of the Sarbanes-Oxley Act of 2002, as amended, so the penalties, along with the disgorgement and prejudgment interest, could be distributed to those harmed by Denha and BKS's conduct described in the Orders.

Human and Computer Trading

It is worth clarifying here that when we use the term "trader" here, we are not necessarily talking about a human being. Historically, humans were the entities that managed a hedge fund's investments. Humans also historically performed all the associated trading and investment operations to support the trading processes. As the computing power of machines has increased, the role of machines in all aspects of hedge fund management has become more pervasive. Many hedge funds utilize specialized computer programs called *algorithms* to implement trading strategies.

An algorithm can be thought of as a set of rules that a computer program is supposed to follow when it is runs. Many algorithms utilized by hedge funds employ artificial intelligence and machine learning techniques. Algorithms can be utilized to perform a wide variety of tasks. Those algorithms that are focused on trading strategies are called *trading algorithms*. Trading algorithms can perform a wide variety of tasks, with often infinitely faster speeds than humans. An example of this would be a new reading algorithm that scans news articles or regulatory filings for information about certain companies and then based on the context of the information uses the algorithm rules to make a trading decision. Other algorithms are utilized to attempt to detect complex market signals and patterns.[9]

Certain hedge fund strategies rely heavily on algorithms to implement complex investment strategies. These types of funds are commonly referred to as *systematic trading funds*, *algorithmic funds* or *quantitative funds*.

In many cases, trading algorithms run on their own subject to human oversight. This means that while a human may be watching what a computer is doing, they are not doing any of the trading themselves. Therefore, the computer algorithm would be populating the pre-trade blotter and then proceeding through the rest of the trading processes we will discuss in this chapter. While the actual implementation varies from among funds, a human may only step in if a certain fund risk limit is approached, such as a fund approaching too large a concentration in a particular position. Oftentimes certain hedge funds utilize algorithms to engage in large volumes of trades over a very short period of time. These strategies are known as *high-frequency trading strategies*, and in the vast majority of cases they trade much faster than any human could. As such, high-frequency trading strategies that employ algorithmic trading are similarly subject to human oversight rather than a human actually implementing the trading strategy.

Chapter Summary

This chapter provided an overview of the subject of trade operations supporting alternative investment funds. We began with a discussion of the types of securities that are traded. Next, we proceeded to discuss the trade idea generation process and contrasted it with trading strategy implementation. We then discussed the process of trade implementation. As part of this process, we outlined the steps in the order entry process, including the use of pre-trade blotters and pre-trade compliance checks. The trade execution process, including the role of brokers, was then discussed. Then we proceeded to cover the trade confirmation, clearing, settlement and reconciliation processes. Finally, we concluded with a discussion of trade allocation and compliance associated trading risks. In the next chapter, we will discuss the role that cash plays in alternative investment operations from supporting trading to expense management.

Notes

1. P. Kiernan, "Commodities Traders Face Limits on Speculative Positions Under U.S. Proposal," *The Wall Street Journal*, January 30, 2020.
2. S. Johnson, "Hedge fund headache," Financial Times, March 8, 2009.
3. J. Kiff, "History of Central Counterparty Failures and Near-Failures, Derivative Prime 7," The OTC Space, available at: https://theotcspace.com/content/history-central-counterparty-failures-and-near-failures-derivative-primer-7.
4. J. Gregory, "Central Counterparties: Mandatory Central Clearing and Initial Margin," Wiley Finance, 2014.

5. Securities and Exchange Commission, "SEC and CFTC Charge Options Clearing Corp. With Failing to Establish and Maintain Adequate Risk Management Policies," September 4, 2019.
6. Securities and Exchange Commission, Release Number 86871, September 4, 2019, available at: https://www.sec.gov/litigation/admin/2019/34-86871.pdf.
7. Commodity Futures Trading Commission, Release Number 7769-18, August 10, 2018, available at: https://www.cftc.gov/PressRoom/PressReleases/7769-18.
8. Securities and Exchange Commission, In the Matter of Reger T. Denha Admin. Proc. File No. 3-18649, August 17, 2018.
9. R. Wigglesworth, "Why hedge fund managers are happy to let the machines take over," *The Financial Times*, October 16, 2019.

3

Cash Management, Oversight and Movement

Introduction to Cash Usage in Alternative Investments

On face value, the concept of cash and its use in alternative investment funds may seem relatively straightforward. Namely, cash is invested by funds to generate profits. Then at some point, investors can take cash out of the fund, hopefully also at a profit. In practice, however, cash is utilized by alternative investment funds for a variety of reasons other than simply making investments and managing investor accounts. This chapter will focus on the uses of cash in alternative investment funds and the operational procedures supporting its uses.

Four Primary Categories of Cash

Alternative investment funds utilize cash for a variety of reasons and in different ways. In practice, there are four primary categories for the ways in which funds dealing with cash can be grouped. They are as follows:

- Cash for expenses
- Cash to facilitate investing
- Cash flow to and from investors
- Unencumbered cash

© The Author(s) 2020
J. Scharfman, *Alternative Investment Operations*,
https://doi.org/10.1007/978-3-030-46629-9_3

Each of these different uses of cash is essential to the management of an alternative investment fund.

Cash Storage Locations

A good starting point for understanding each of the four primary uses of cash is to first understand the sources of cash. Once we have established the source of cash in different operational procedures, we can then analyze how the cash flows through the fund entities and, finally, how the cash is ultimately utilized. Before we can begin this analysis however, we first need to cover some basics about alternative investment fund structures.

Master-Feeder Structure

In this most simple form, an alternative investment fund consists of four entities. The first in this simple model is known as the *management company*. The management company is simply a legal entity that is controlled by one or more individuals or affiliated with the fund manager. Practically, it can be thought of as the corporation for which employees such as portfolio managers, investment analysts and operations personnel work for while facilitating the investment activities of the funds.

The second entity would be the actual investment fund that does the investing. It should be noted that technically the funds managed by an alternative investment fund are effectively overseen by an entity known as *General Partner (GP)* of the fund, which would be the third entity involved in this complex. Although there is often a technical legal distinction in place between the GP and the alternative investment management company, in practice the term "GP" is also utilized synonymously. In many cases, there is also an entity known as an investment manager that is the entity that is technically responsible for managing the investments of the fund. You may recall from Chap. 2 that an investment fund is also commonly referred to as an investment vehicle, or simply vehicle. In practice, the investment vehicle is commonly a domestic investment vehicle which would be located in the same country as the management company. This relationship is summarized in Fig. 3.1. In practice, an example of this would be a hedge fund with an office in New York City that is incorporated for legal purposes in the state of Delaware and manages a fund that is also domiciled in Delaware.

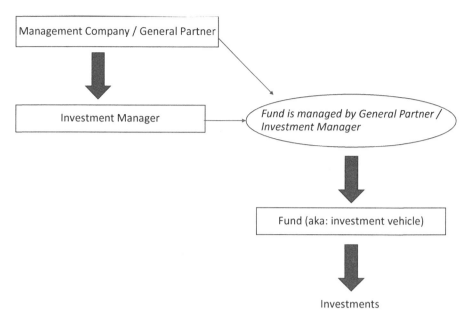

Fig. 3.1 Simple Alternative Investment Fund Structure

In Chap. 2, we introduced the concept of onshore and offshore investment vehicles. For reference, these are effectively different versions of the same fund that invest in substantially the same manner. The difference is the domicile of where each fund is established in order to facilitate the needs and tax considerations of different investors. A variation on the simple model would be for a fund manager to maintain onshore and offshore funds that simply make direct investments themselves which pursuing the same material investment strategy. This is referred to as a *side-by-side structure* or *paripassu structure*.

Another common alternative investment fund structure is known as *a master-feeder structure*. In a master-feeder structure, the onshore and offshore funds feed their capital into a master fund. This master fund then makes investments on behalf of the feeder funds. In this way, while the different needs of onshore and offshore investors are satisfied, the trading of the fund is consolidated at the master fund level in a single trading entity.

It should be noted that while the feeder funds typically allocate the majority of their capital to the master fund, they often technically have the ability to make their own feeder fund-level investments as well. For this reason, each feeder fund maintains separate *books and records* for tax and financial reporting purposes from the master fund. Performance fees and management fees are also typically charged at the feeder fund levels directly as opposed to the master fund level and then allocated down to the feeders.

Additionally, it should be noted that in a master-feeder structure each fund will have a designated general partner and investment manager. While these are typically the same entity, the point is that each fund in the overall master-feeder complex designates its own general partner and investment manager where applicable. Figure 3.2 provides an example of a master-feeder structure.

For reference there is a different modified version of the master-feeder structure called a *mini master-feeder structure*. In this framework, there are usually two entities: an offshore feeder and a master. Similar to the master-feeder structure, a key motivation of this structure are tax consequences, and a mini-master feeder may be more advantageous for certain fund managers as opposed to the full master-feeder structure. The onshore fund in a mini-master feeder case would simply be a stand-alone fund outside of the mini-master feeder structure, and therefore the onshore fund would not feed into the master.

Cash Accounts for Different Funds

Now that we have provided an overview of two examples of common alternative investment fund models (i.e. simple and master-feeder), we can next

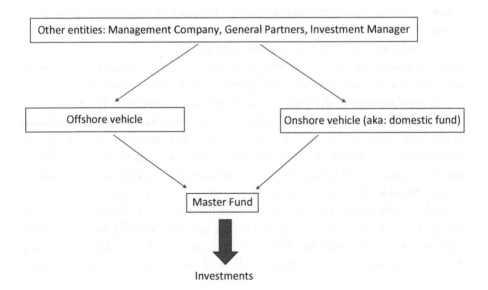

Fig. 3.2 Master-Feeder Alternative Investment Fund Structure

consider the storage locations of cash. In practice, each investment vehicle maintains a separate bank account in the name of the respective fund. Depending on the nature of the structure cash would then be moved among the different funds respective bank accounts to accomplish different goals. Separately, a fund's management company typically maintains a separate operating bank account.

Cash for Expenses

Returning to the list of four primary categories of cash usage, the first category is cash for fund expenses. This type of cash is referred to as *expense cash* and is utilized is to pay the expenses of the funds and management company. Both entities incur many different types of expenses. Some of these expenses are primarily related to the investment activities of the fund. Examples of these type of expenses would include trading and investment research costs.

Investment expenses can be compared to those expenses that are primarily focused on the non-investment and operational aspects of hedge funds. These are called *operational expenses* and can include items such as regularly recurring expenses such as the audit bills of a fund. Operational expenses could also include costs related to other operational items such as legal expenses and compliance costs.

Some expenses are combination of investment and operational expenses. These are called *blended expenses*. An example of a blended expense would be information technology–related costs. This is a blended expense because a computer server, for example, can be utilized to both facilitate a hedge fund's trading activities and assist in making regulatory filings on the operational side. Expense cash can be either paid to third parties or allocated internally to different vehicles and entities within the hedge fund. This is the reason that it's important to classify expenses as either investment, operational or blended because different types of expenses may be allocated to different hedge fund vehicles or entities.

Expense Policies

It is important to note that there are not always clear rules with regards to how expenses will be allocated. Some fund expenses may be paid at the individual fund level, whereas other funds could be paid by the management company. In many cases, it is in the discretion of the fund manager. This discretion, however, must be accompanied with transparency. To provide this clarity on the anticipated treatment of fund expenses, a fund manager typically develops a document called an *expense policy*. This policy will outline the general anticipated treatment of fund expenses, including which expenses will be charged to the investment manager as compared to the funds as well as any allocation of shared expenses.

It should be noted that while it would be considered best practice from an operational perspective for a fund manager to maintain a stand-alone allocation policy, in other cases the fund manager may rely on expense language contained in the *offering memorandum* of a fund. In practice, the offering memorandum is often abbreviated as OM. This offering memorandum, which is also referred to as a *private placement memorandum*, is a document that is provided to investors prior to investing in a fund that outlines a number of key considerations and risks related to making an investment in a fund. For reference, in practice the private placement memorandum is often abbreviated as PPM. Following is an example of a portion of the expense language contained in a fund PPM that also addresses organizational cost expenses:

The Fund will be responsible for, and on an ongoing basis will pay, all of its Operating Expenses. The Operating Expenses include:

(1) legal, accounting, administrative, auditing, consulting, tax preparation, and similar fees and expenses;
(2) out-of-pocket expenses of Advisory Committee members in connection with their meetings and other activities in such capacity, and of the meetings, if any, of the Partners;
(3) out-of-pocket expenses associated with attracting, sourcing, identifying, researching, and evaluating potential Fund Investments, including fees for data licensing, investment models, or other metrics, due diligence, and sourcing- and diligence-related travel costs, the ongoing oversight, holding, and Disposition of Fund Investments, and any broken-deal or other fees and expenses associated with potential Fund Investments, to the extent not paid by the applicable borrower or other issuer of, or the seller of, the applicable Fund Investment or other applicable counterparty;
(4) insurance (including errors and omissions insurance of the General Partner, the Investment Manager, their respective Affiliates, and/or the Advisory Committee members), litigation, and indemnification expenses;
(5) taxes, fees, and other governmental charges levied against the Fund; and
(6) costs and expenses corresponding to the foregoing arising from, and any organizational and start-up expenses relating to the formation of, any sub-

sidiary entities formed or acquired in connection with making Fund
Investments.

To the extent that any Operating Expenses are incurred on behalf of the Fund
and other investment entities or accounts managed by the General Partner, the
Investment Manager, or their respective Affiliates, such expenses shall be allocated among the Fund and the other applicable entities and/or accounts on an
equitable basis, as determined by the General Partner in its sole discretion. For
the avoidance of doubt, the Fund will bear, in their entirety, any expenses
incurred in connection with unconsummated co-investment opportunities,
including those expenses that would have been allocable to the other Co-Investors
had the relevant co-investment opportunity been consummated.

Organizational Expenses:

The Fund will be responsible for paying all Organizational Expenses
that include:

(1) all costs and expenses incurred in connection with the organization of the
Fund (including legal fees and disbursements associated with the preparation of the Fund's organizational documentation, fees and other expenses
incurred in connection with the formation and registration of the Fund in
Delaware and with the registration of the Fund in each jurisdiction where
it has qualified to do business in connection with the commencement of its
operations, and taxes, duties, and other similar expenses associated with the
establishment of the Fund);

(2) all costs and expenses incurred in connection with the offering and sale of
Interests (including legal fees and disbursements associated with the preparation of this Memorandum and any other marketing materials for the
Fund and to amend or supplement this Memorandum or such other marketing materials; fees and expenses of legal counsel and other advisers
incurred in connection with negotiation of side letters with existing and
prospective Limited Partners; but excluding any placement fees, commis-
sions, and expenses of third-party marketers retained to solicit investments
into the Fund);

(3) all costs and expenses incurred in connection with the preparation and
execution of the Fund's contracts required for it to commence its operations; and

(4) all expenses incurred in connection with the organization of the General
Partner.

For financial reporting purposes, the Organizational Expenses will be amor-
tized over a 60-month period beginning on the Initial Closing Date, unless

otherwise provided in the Partnership Agreement or determined by the General Partner. Although such amortization of Organizational Expenses is a divergence from GAAP, it is not expected to result in a qualification of the Fund's annual audited financial statements.

It is worth noting that in the above example language from a PPM, despite being a deviation from US Generally Accepted Accounting Principles (US GAAP), the amortization of organizational expenses over a 60-month (i.e. five-year) period is standard in the alternative investment fund industry.

To illustrate how expense policies work in practice, let us consider the rent expense incurred by the fund manager in order to provide its employees with a space from which to manage investments. Should the management company bear this expense entirely? Perhaps it would also be fair for the individual investment vehicles to pay for a portion of this rent? On the one hand, the management company earns a management fee the historical purpose of it to be utilized for administrative costs such as payroll and rent. On the other hand, all of the space rented by a management company may not be utilized for a specific fund and instead may be utilized for more general firm activities, such as firm-wide meetings. Additionally, the office space that is rented could be used to conduct research for multiple different investment strategies and funds managed by the firm. In practice, office rent is typically paid entirely by the management company and is not an expense that is shared by the funds.

Other expenses, however, may be entirely passed on to the fund vehicles themselves as opposed to being covered by the management company. These expenses are then effectively passed on to a fund's investors, and as such are referred to as *pass thru expenses*. A common pass thru expense in the hedge fund industry is the cost of a third-party service provider known as a fund administrator. Administrators perform a variety of tasks including assisting with trade reconciliation, as we discussed in Chap. 2, as well as investor services and reporting. For reference, the role of fund administrators is discussed in more detail in Chap. 5.

Cash Movement for Expenses

To illustrate how cash is utilized and moved for expenses, let us consider the movement of cash for expenses in a master-feeder fund structure. In a traditional master-feeder structure, all purchases, sales, interest and dividends earned are recorded at the master fund level. The master fund then allocates the respective percentages of profit and loss to feeder funds with respect to the

Table 3.1   Master-Feeder Fund Expense Recording Summary

Fund type	Recorded at this fund level	Bank account expenses paid from	Net effect
Master fund	All purchases, sales, interest and dividends earned are recorded at the master fund level	Master fund bank account	Profit and loss components allocated back to feeder fund(s)
Feeder funds (onshore and offshore)	Expenses and liabilities related to direct feeder investments and feeder-specific liabilities and organizational expenses	Feeder fund bank account.[a]	Expenses paid from feeder fund bank accounts

[a]*Note:* Each feeder fund has its own separate bank account in the name of the feeder fund

appropriate economic percentages each feeder fund is owed. At the feeder level, there may be specific feeder-level expenses as well. Examples of these include those related to direct feeder investments, as well as feeder-specific liabilities and organizational expenses. To pay these feeder-level expenses, cash would be sourced from the feeder-level bank account. Table 3.1 provides a summary of this relationship.

Let us consider next the example of a hedge fund with a third-party administrator seeking to pay a feeder-level bill from an accounting firm for tax consulting services related to this specific feeder. The first step in the process would be for the vendor, in this case the accounting firm, to send an invoice to the hedge fund. This invoice typically would be sent to the accounting department at the hedge fund management company.

Once the invoice is received, it would next be reviewed by the hedge fund management company for accuracy. If there are any discrepancies with regards to the amount of the invoice, then the hedge fund accounting department would work with the accounting firm to resolve these discrepancies. If there are no issues, or after any issues have been resolved, the next step would be for the hedge fund manager to approve the invoice.

After approval, the hedge fund manager would then need to make a determination as to what sources of cash should be utilized to pay this invoice. This is often where the fund managers expense policy comes into play. In some cases, it is clear as to what sources of cash should be used to pay this invoice based on the expense policy. As noted above, if the invoice is from the hedge fund's landlord in order to pay rent, then we have established that according to most hedge fund expense policies, and as is standard industry practice, this would be an expense of the management company and not of any of the fund vehicles. On the other hand, bills for fund administration are traditionally fund-level expenses. As noted above, some other expenses may require more discretion on the managers party in order to determine the sources of funds and if any expenses should be split up among various entities, and in what percentages this division of expenses should occur. For these types of situations, where the allocation of expenses among different entities and funds is required, the next step in the process after approval would typically be for the fund manager to document the ways in which the expenses are being allocated. This could be memorialized in an *expense allocation memorandum* that would then be signed off on by senior personnel in the firm such as the chief financial officer, chief operating officer or chief investment officer.

Continuing our example, next the hedge fund would then send a copy of the invoice to the fund administrator for review. In practice, the hedge fund may have an arrangement in place with vendors so that when an invoice is sent to the hedge fund, they also send a copy at the same time to the administrator. The point here is that in our example in the sequential process of fund expense review, approval and payment, at this stage typically the administrator would not begin their review until after the invoice is approved by the hedge fund.

This is an important step for several reasons. Firstly, the fund administrator typically is responsible for maintaining the books and records of each specific fund that it administers. Therefore, if a feeder fund was going to make a payment, the administrator would need to be apprised of this fact so that it could maintain accurate records of any payments made. Practically, this administrator review of the accounting invoice also adds an additional level of independent review to the process so that the hedge fund management company alone is not the sole reviewer.

Similar to the review process undertaken by the hedge fund manager, the administrator will conduct their own review of the invoice to determine if there are any discrepancies to be resolved. If there are, then these issues will be investigated with the hedge fund manager and accounting firm vendor. Once these are resolved, or once again if there are no issues, then the administrator would then approve the invoice from their side.

Once this second level of approval has been granted, then the administrator would typically instruct the feeder fund bank to initiate payment of the invoice. In some cases, the fund bank may double check that payment is indeed intended to be made with the hedge fund manager prior to releasing the funds. Once the funds are released, the invoice is marked as paid and the expense payment process for this invoice would be complete.

It should be noted that the process we just described above is not set in stone. Different alternative investment fund managers may employ different forms of this process. As we will discuss in Chap. 8, many private equity managers do not utilize third-party administrator. If they do, the ways in which they utilize them is typically different than their hedge fund counterparts. As such, the ways cash is transferred through this process might be significantly different for private equity firms versus hedge funds. Additionally, even within the group of hedge funds that utilize third-party administrators, as opposed to self-administering their own funds, there could be substantial differences in the specific practices employed in the movement of cash and the process utilized to pay expenses. The point is that each specific fund manager has discretion to employ slightly different versions of the same process while transferring cash for fund expenses, but a key takeaway to remember is that specific feeder-level expenses are paid from the specific feeder-level bank accounts and not netted at the master fund level. The steps in the above described process are summarized in Fig. 3.3.

Cash To Facilitate Trading

The second type of cash out of the four primary categories is the cash that is utilized to facilitate trading and making investments. Cash utilized in this way is referred to as *investment cash*. For reference, the trading process we discussed in Chap. 2 would not be able to function if a fund doesn't have the cash to actually fund the trade. In a trade cash transfers from one party to another in exchange for the subject of the trade (i.e. securities). In some cases, a fund is a buyer of a security and transfers cash to the other party in exchange for the securities. In other cases, a fund is a seller and receives cash in exchange for securities given to another party.

To illustrate how this would work in practice, let us consider a hedge fund seeking to execute a trade. Let us further assume for the purposes of our example that there is a master-feeder fund structure in place. The first step in the process would be for the feeder funds to transfer cash to the master fund for trading. As noted in the previous section, the feeder funds can indeed execute trades at the feeder level but for this example let us assume that the particular trade we are focused on takes place at the master fund level.

After the cash is transferred to the master fund, now it is time to execute the trade. If the fund is executing a straightforward purchase of a publicly traded stock, then the trading process described in Chap. 2 would proceed whereby the fund would work with a prime broker to execute a trade with a

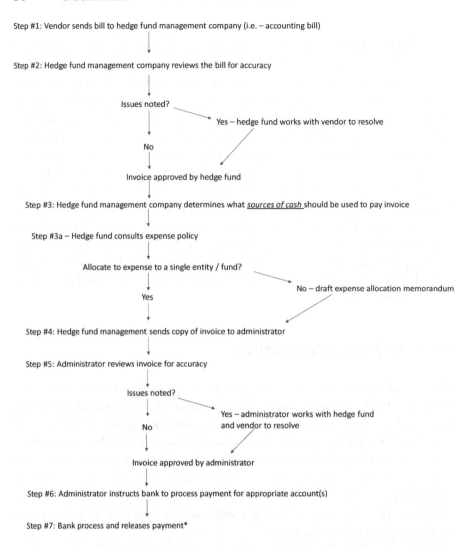

Step #1: Vendor sends bill to hedge fund management company (i.e. – accounting bill)

Step #2: Hedge fund management company reviews the bill for accuracy

Issues noted?

Yes – hedge fund works with vendor to resolve

No

Invoice approved by hedge fund

Step #3: Hedge fund management company determines what *sources of cash* should be used to pay invoice

Step #3a – Hedge fund consults expense policy

Allocate to expense to a single entity / fund?

No – draft expense allocation memorandum

Yes

Step #4: Hedge fund management sends copy of invoice to administrator

Step #5: Administrator reviews invoice for accuracy

Issues noted?

Yes – administrator works with hedge fund and vendor to resolve

No

Invoice approved by administrator

Step #6: Administrator instructs bank to process payment for appropriate account(s)

Step #7: Bank process and releases payment*

Fig. 3.3 Example Approval and Cash Movement Process for Expense Payment (Hedge Fund using master-feeder structure with Third-Party Administrator)

counterparty. Upon settlement, cash would be transferred from the master fund's bank account to the prime broker to fund the trade. In return the prime broker would provide the fund with the stock.

For other types of trades such as options and futures trades that require margin deposits cash to facilitate trading, cash may have to be placed with an exchange, posted as margin or provided as collateral. In these cases, the fund's cash for trading is sitting with another party or intermediaries temporarily. Even though the cash may only be there temporarily until the trade is complete, the hedge fund is still exposed from a counterparty perspective to this party. That is to say, if the counterparty fails the hedge fund's cash may be at risk of being lost. This is referred to as *counterparty risk*. As such, the fund should take measures to evaluate the overall credit quality of fund counterparties on an initial and ongoing basis.

Cash Sweeping Frequency

Related to counterparty risk concerns for cash trading is the concept of sweeping cash. When we say that cash is swept by a fund, we mean it is called back by the fund from a counterparty. Think of it as the hedge fund holding a broom and sweeping the back into its own accounts. When hedge funds enter into certain types of transactions that require margin posting, they may have an ongoing cash balance left over with a counterparty or intermediary such as a prime broker at the end of the trading day. The hedge fund has two options at this point. The first option is to just leave the cash sitting there in its account at the counterparty overnight since it will likely continue to trade tomorrow and need cash for margin in its account. The downside of this approach is that it exposes the fund to counterparty risk, as noted above. Additionally, the fund would be forgoing any overnight short-term interest that could be earned on the cash. The second approach would be for the hedge fund to sweep back the cash from counterparties. It is considered best practice in most cases for the fund to do this on a nightly basis to remove the counterparty risks associated with leaving the cash overnight, as well as afford the fund with the opportunity to earn interest on this cash.

Cash To and From Investors

The third type of cash out of the four primary categories is the cash that is transferred to and from investors into an alternative investment fund. When a fund first starts, it must obtain money to do its investing from somewhere. This money can come from two primary sources. The first is from sources internal to the fund management company such as the portfolio manager and the fund management company's employees themselves. This is called *proprietary capital.*

The second type of capital comes from sources that are external to the fund manager. For a newly launched fund, typically a large capital allocation from a single investor or group of investors, referred to as *anchor investors*, is used to get the fund going. This investment is referred to as *seed capital*. In most cases, a fund receives capital from both internal and external sources. The combined group of capital is referred to as a *pool of capital*. This pool of capital is then invested by the fund.

When a fund receives capital coming in, also called *inflows* or subscriptions, this process is referred to as the *subscription process*. In practice, a fund will establish a bank account with which to receive these subscriptions. The process will generally begin with an investor submitting cash via a process called a *wire* or *cash wire*. The wire process involves the investor instructing their own bank to transfer capital to the fund's bank account. Subscriptions may also be made via a physical check. In many cases, a fund manager may work with a *fund administrator*, to assist in facilitating the paperwork and forms associated with processing the subscription.

The other side of the subscription process is when a fund transfers capital from the fund back to investors. This process is called an *outflow of capital* or *redemption*. A redemption effectively works in the opposite way of a subscription. The redemption process typically begins with an investor submitting a written request, called a *redemption notice*, to a fund. The redemption notice indicates that the investors desire to withdraw capital from the fund. If a fund works with a third-party administrator, then the administrator will often be involved in the processing of the paperwork to determine that the appropriate entities are being paid capital to the correct accounts.

While we are on the topic of redemptions, it should also be noted that in the vast majority of instances it is anticipated that an investor will receive their redemption proceeds in cash. There is, however, an option outlined in the offering documents of a fund such as the *private placement memoranda* of many fund managers that allows for something known as an *in-kind redemption*. Under an in-kind redemption, a fund manager has the ability to pay the investor not in cash but in securities equivalent to the value of the redemption. The manager often has a great deal of discretion, if not total say, with regards to the actual types of securities used to satisfy the redemption. For example, they could range from highly liquid securities to thinly traded or even illiquid securities.

Unencumbered Cash

The fourth type of cash out of the four primary categories is *unencumbered cash*. Unencumbered cash is the cash that a hedge fund has on hand that it has not designated for another purpose. Examples of unencumbered cash could be:

- New cash from investors that the fund has not yet designated for investment
- Cash that a fund has earned from the sale of securities that has not been reinvested
- Leftover cash from daily trading operations

A fund has a few different options with regards to how to utilize this cash. The first option is to do nothing and leave the cash in whatever account it is sitting in. A second option would be for a fund to gather this unencumbered cash together, a process known as *pooling cash*. Once pooled, the fund could then invest then place this cash into a placeholder vehicle that earns interest. The purpose of pooling cash as opposed to making several individual deposits is that the fund can make a larger single cash deposit and, therefore, likely earn more favorable interest rates based on the larger amount.

While many funds' primary purpose is not to earn money on unencumbered cash, and instead to focus on earning profits from their investments, funds have also recognized increasingly that they have a responsibility to not just let this cash sit around but rather maximize its value in a counterparty risk-sensitive way. It should be noted that not every fund actively manages cash and some just leave cash overnight with counterparties or in noninterest-bearing accounts, such as savings accounts. Some funds may not feel it is worth the extra effort to earn interest on cash. Others may also feel that there is not significant counterparty risk, and, therefore, from a risk management perspective calling back cash may not be a priority to them. That being said, it is considered best practice in most instances for a fund to actively manage unencumbered cash.

One option would be for a fund to deposit the cash into a relatively straightforward cash management vehicle such as an interest-bearing savings account. Another option, which may generate more interest, would be for the fund to invest in overnight money market funds that invest in cash and cash equivalents such as government treasuries and municipal securities. A fund may also work with a third party to assist in pooling and managing cash. This is not without its own counterparty risk arising from the third-party cash manager.

One example of this was the failure of a well-known hedge fund cash manager called Sentinel Management Group based in Illinois, the United States, which in August 2007 failed due to fraud. When Sentinel failed, many hedge funds which had cash balances with them found that they could no longer access what they thought was liquid cash, and this significantly disrupted their ability to function and trade. Similarly, when the Lehman Brothers failed in 2008, many hedge funds that had utilized Lehman Brothers as a prime broker and were not vigilant about sweeping cash back from trading accounts and monitoring counterparty risk found themselves in a similar situation of not being able to function with their cash frozen out at Lehman.

Cash Controls

Earlier in the chapter in our discussion of cash for expenses, we outlined that various levels of reviews often take place within the hedge fund management company prior to approving the movement of cash for expenses. In the majority of cases, various levels of internal review are similarly employed with regards to the movement of other types of cash including investment cash, paying out cash redemptions and unencumbered cash. This process of oversight of the movement of cash is referred to as the *cash control process*.

The primary purpose of a cash control process is to ensure that cash is not utilized for the proper purposes. One example of the misuse of cash could be outright embezzlement where an employee steals cash for themselves. In other instances, however, operational clerical errors could occur that, for example, cause the wrong amounts of cash to be transferred for legitimate purposes simply due to manual error. Alternatively, the correct amount of cash could be transferred for a legitimate purpose, but it is transferred from the wrong fund account or perhaps paid to the wrong vendor. These types of instances are much more common than outright employee theft in most cases, and, therefore, the cash control process serves as an operational risk management tool in addition to overseeing more extreme instances of theft and fraud.

Cash Initiators and Approvers

While every fund manager will likely have different nuances to their own cash management process, there are certain procedures in a cash control process that are considered best practice. The first is that the initiator of the cash transfer should be different than the approver. An *initiator* in this context means the person who begins the cash transfer process. Multiple people in a fund may have the authority to initiate a cash transfer but initiation of an individual cash transfer is commonly only performed by one individual at a time. Additionally, to be clear this does not mean that they are the one generating the trade request or vendor invoice for example, that is, the reason for the cash being requested. No, in this case the role of the initiator is effectively to step in after the reason for the cash being needed has been established and set up the appropriate paperwork so that the cash transfer review process can begin. Different funds utilize different procedures for cash initiation. In the case of a vendor invoice for example, the initiator would receive the invoice, either typically via email or physical mail. Then they would log the invoice. Historically, this logging process may have taken place in physical form such as a physical accounting ledger. Today, this logging process would generally involve entering the invoice into a fund accounting system. To clarify, some funds may maintain their own in-house fund accounting systems, while others may not maintain in-house systems but instead rely on the accounting systems of third-party service providers such as a fund administrator.

After the initiator sets up the cash transfer request, the next step in the process would be for it to be reviewed by an approver. An *approver* is an individual that is responsible for granting authority for a cash transfer to proceed. In some cases, a fund manager may have multiple approvers in place and funds employ different approval frameworks. A key point to note at this stage is that it is considered best practice for the initiator of a cash transfer and the approver to be different people. The purpose for this is so that a single individual does not control both aspects of the cash transfer process. If a single person did control both aspects of the process, they could simply initiate a fraudulent payment to themselves, or a friend, and then approve it to themselves with no oversight. Eventually, the payment may be caught during reviews such as audits but there would likely be a significant delay between the fraudulent payment and the theft. Even worse, the theft could never be caught.

Single Initiator Approver Model

Outside of fraud considerations, it is also considered best practice to have at least two separate individuals involved in the two stages of the cash transfer process in order to provide operational oversight for non-fraudulent errors. For example, consider if an invoice from a vendor requested a payment of $432 but the initiator made a clerical transposition error and set up the payment request in the fund accounting system for $423. This error then reversed the numbers "2" and "3" in the figure, and if approved as is would result in a shortfall to the vendor of $9. If the same person who was the initiator was the approver, then you see how unlikely it would be that the same individual would catch their own mistake. This is another flaw of the *single initiator approver model*.

Cash Threshold Model

Despite these flaws, historically some funds have taken the approach that transfers of cash in smaller amounts do not require a separate approval at all and can be functionally approved by the initiator. This is referred to as a *cash threshold model*. To be clear, this is not to imply that the fund does not utilize or maintain any separate individuals who are approvers of cash transfers. Rather, the approvers are only required to grant approvals when the amount of the cash transfers exceeds a certain threshold level. As discussed above, the use of the single initiator approver model is not considered best practice; however, the reasoning for funds that used a single initiator approver is that they incorrectly feel the overall risk to the firm based on the small amount of cash involved is offset by the operational efficiency of only having one step involved in the process as opposed to multiple people. Functionally, the cash transfer must still go through the initiator step (i.e. being set up in the fund accounting system) and then the approval step (i.e. approved in the accounting system); however, the actual person doing the initiating and subsequent approving would be the same. The way this would work in practice would be that a fund would establish some arbitrary level that they feel was an appropriate cutoff from a risk reward trade-off perspective. Figure 3.4 demonstrates the example of how this process would work with a $10,000 threshold level. As demonstrated in Fig. 3.4, the way the $10,000 threshold works is that for cash transfers under $10,000 no other approvals would be required but for invoices over $10,000 another approver would be required that would be different than the negotiator.

It is also worth noting that some funds may try to compromise on this cash threshold model by allowing a single initiator and approver for amount under the threshold only to *pre-approved vendors*. These are vendors with whom the firm has an ongoing relationship and, therefore, has decided to apply a lower level of scrutiny to cash payments made to these vendors. For example, consider that a hedge fund has worked with the same law firm for many years. Let us further assume that the law firm regularly bills the fund $5000 a quarter for corporate secretary services. The fund in our example also utilizes a

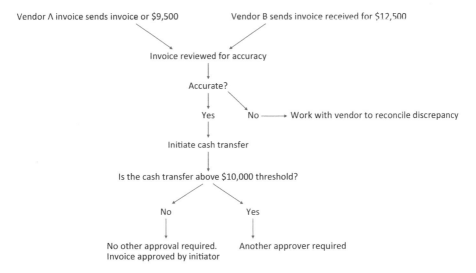

Fig. 3.4 Single Initiator Approval Model With $10,000 Threshold

$10,000 cash approval threshold. In this case, under a compromise approach a fund may decide to allow payments under $10,000 to regularly preapproved vendors such as the law firm in our example. The reasoning behind this approach is that if the vendor is preapproved, it effectively eliminates the possibility that a person at the fund could create a fraudulent invoice and then facilitate payment to an unauthorized payee.

A key point of consideration with such a model is the question of who controls the preapproved vendor list. One area where there is potential for dangerous control oversight in this regard is that the list of preapproved vendors might be formally approved by a more senior fund professional such as the chief operating officer (COO) or chief financial officer (CFO); however, in practice, more junior personnel may have the ability to add new vendors. If there are not strict controls, then the list could be manipulated to create fraudulent cash transfers.

Let us consider the example of a hedge fund where there is a single individual, Mr. Smith, who is both the initiator and the approver of cash transfers under $10,000 made to preapproved vendors. Transfers over the $10,000 threshold require approval by a separate individual. Also, let us assume that Mr. Smith functionally controls the preapproved list of vendors subject to limited oversight by his supervisors. One example of the way such a scheme would work in practice is that Mr. Smith could create a new vendor, which in actuality does nothing but controls, and add them on the preapproved list. He would then create a real bank account in the name of the fraudulent vendor. Next, Mr. Smith could then create an invoice from this fraudulent vendor for an amount under the $10,000 threshold, say $5500. He would then simply initiate a payment to the fraudulent vendor's bank account, which he in actuality controls, and then embezzle the funds for himself.

Another variation on this scheme would be for Mr. Smith to select a vendor with whom they do not have a direct relationship, such as an accounting firm owned by Mr. Smith's brother. In this case, the accounting firm is a real company, not a manufactured one as in the previous example. However, there is no actual legitimate business between the accounting firm and the fund. Similar to the method employed in the previous example, Mr. Smith would simply add the accounting firm to the preapproved vendor list. An invoice would then be submitted by the accounting firm under the threshold level, say for $9900, with the knowledge that it will be incorrectly paid by Mr. Smith who is also in on the scheme.

Let us continue our example but let us change the framework to say that the fund has now implemented more stringent controls over the preapproved list than the one in our previous example, but still employs a single initiator and approver with a $10,000 threshold. Would it be possible for Mr. Smith to still manage to steal money in this case? The answer is yes. A common fraudulent scheme that could be perpetrated under this scenario would be for Mr. Smith to convince a legitimate vendor of the firm to *bill for services never performed* and share in the stolen funds with them. In this case, the vendor could submit invoices for services never rendered but that would still be able to be approved solely by Mr. Smith because the vendor was on the preapproved list as long as the invoices were all under the $10,000 threshold level. Alternatively, a preapproved vendor could *overbill for services* by submitting legitimate invoices for services that were indeed performed but increase the amount that should have correctly been charged. For example, let us assume that a preapproved law firm did $4500 of legitimate legal work for a fund. The vendor, who is participating in the overbilling scheme in coordination with Mr. Smith, could submit the bill for $7500 instead, an overbilling of $3000. Since this is still under the $10,000 threshold and the vendor is on the preapproved list, Mr. Smith could then simply approve the invoice and share in the $300 amount overbilled with the vendor.

Ultimately, the vast majority of fund employees are well intentioned people and not prone to theft; however, thefts and simple operational mistakes do occur for a variety of reasons, and when lax operational cash controls provide the opportunity for these thefts and errors to occur, it can create a variety of problems for fund managers. This is why it is essential that cash controls are designed and tested to ensure that there is appropriate independent oversight throughout the initiation and approvals process for cash transfers.

Different Initiator Approver With No Threshold Model

The risks associated with both single initiator approver model and the cash threshold model are not worth any efficiency trade-offs recouped. For these reasons, in addition to having a separate initiator and approver for cash transfers, it is also considered a better operational practice for all cash transfers to require approval regardless of the amount of the transfer. This is considered best practice because it solves the problem of having a single initiator and approver and also resolves threshold considerations. Practically, if we consider this in a cash threshold model context, the threshold would therefore be zero.

This can be referred to as the *different initiator approver with no threshold model*. This model can be further approved upon by requiring multiple different approvers. The use of multiple approvers for cash transfers can function in a few different ways. One approach would be that at least two approvers are required for all cash transfers. The general thinking behind a multiple approver approach is that the more independent people you have reviewing a transaction, the more likely you are to have any errors caught before the cash is transferred. Additionally, the more people involved in a process, the more complicated it is to orchestrate a fraud or embezzlement scheme because there are practically more people that need to be involved in it.

Chapter Summary

This chapter provided an overview of the cash management, oversight and movement processes. It began with an introduction to the four primary categories of cash: cash for expenses, cash to facilitate investing, cash flow to and from investors and unencumbered cash. It then proceeded to discuss each category as well as cash storage locations and common fund structures employed including the master-feeder structure. As part of this discussion, we also outlined the role of onshore and offshore feeder funds and side-by-side structures. Next, it discussed fund expense policies and procedures in more detail. It then discussed cash control procedures and best practices for funds. In the next chapter, we will discuss compliance operations and governance considerations.

4

Compliance Operations and Governance Considerations

Introduction to Compliance Operations and Governance Considerations

Historically, in the alternative investment fund industry the compliance function was a separate and distinct area of firm operations as compared to the more traditional back office accounting and finance operations functions. Today, in the modern alternative investment fund there is a greatly increased coordination and integration of the compliance function into the larger operational functions of the firm.

There are several practical reasons why compliance and operations have become increasingly connected. In part, the motivation for this integration is due to necessity. Firstly, compliance management across the entire investment industry has grown in scope and complexity in recent years. With this increase in compliance challenges has come a need for more data regarding fund operations in order to successfully implement compliance oversight throughout a firm. Secondly, the speed at which this operational data must be produced has also increased greatly in recent years. Finally, increasingly regulators are requesting new and different types of data from fund managers than they have in the past. Compliance relies on operations to provide access this data for reporting purposes. To begin our discussion of compliance, we can outline the role of the compliance function. On a high level, the role of the compliance function in an alternative investment fund can be divided into two primary areas: mandatory compliance and voluntary compliance.

© The Author(s) 2020
J. Scharfman, *Alternative Investment Operations*,
https://doi.org/10.1007/978-3-030-46629-9_4

Mandatory Compliance

The first area deals with what is known as *mandatory compliance*. These are the compliance rules that an alternative investment manager is required to follow. More specifically, mandatory compliance can be divided into two subcategories of mandatory rules. The first set are those that arise based on the location of the alternative investment managers offices, employees and affiliates. We will refer to these as *location-based mandatory compliance rules*. One example of these types of location-based rules would be the laws in the country in which an alternative investment fund is headquartered. For countries such as the United States with many different states, these may also be applicable to laws at the state level, which could be mandatory for a fund manager to comply with. A common example of such an arrangement would be a New York City–based private equity fund manager, that is, it has its primary office and employees in New York City, but the general partner entity is incorporated in the state of Delaware.

An alternative investment fund may also have satellite offices in other countries, which may also be subject to specific mandatory requirements that may differ from the home countries' compliance rules. Additionally, alternative investment fund manager may also conduct business in countries in which it does not have any offices or employees. A common example of a scenario where this could occur would be a US-based hedge fund manager conducting marketing activities in Switzerland. In this case, the US fund would be subject to mandatory compliance rules with regards to its US operation as well as any specific mandatory compliance rules regarding marketing and fund-raising in Switzerland.

The second set of mandatory compliance rules come about as a result of the alternative investment fund activities. We will refer to these as *activity-based mandatory compliance rules*. The most straightforward example of activity-based rules would be mandatory compliance obligations resulting from a fund investment activity. For example, consider a hedge fund that trades in US futures. This trading activity would in future would likely trigger certain compliance obligations for the fund as administered by the Commodity Futures Trading Commission (CFTC) and the National Futures Association (NFA). Compare this to a different hedge fund that only traded in Japanese equities. Instead of being required to follow CFTC and NFA compliance rules, this fund would instead be subject to Japanese Financial Services Agency.

It should also be noted that certain activities of alternative investment funds are both location- and activity based. An example of this was the situation discussed earlier in which a US-based hedge fund was marketing in Switzerland. In this case, the Swiss location of the activity is triggering certain compliance obligations. Concurrently, the specific activity in question (i.e. marketing) is also triggering separate compliance obligations, and these mandatory compliance obligations would be different as compared to, for example, if the hedge fund was making investments in Switzerland and opposed to conducting marketing activities there.

Sources of Mandatory Compliance Rules

The rules for mandatory compliance come from two primary sources. The first source is from *legislation*. Legislation refers to the laws that impact the activities, both investment and operational, of alternative investment managers. Legislation comes from entities known as legislative bodies. These legislative bodies include groups such as Parliament in the United Kingdom and the US Congress.

The second source of mandatory compliance rules comes from what is known as *regulatory implementation*. Once legislation is passed into law by financial regulators, it then must be actually enacted in the real-world marketplace. Regulators commonly utilize a process called rulemaking to further craft the specifics required to implement legislation. This is especially true for legislation that is very technical in nature in its implementation. Additionally, once the first round of a new legislation has been implemented, there is often feedback from the market that is requested by regulators with regards to problems or challenges that may have arisen in the implementation of a new law through a process known as *rulemaking*.

Voluntary Compliance

The second area of compliance deals with what is known as *voluntary compliance*. These are the compliance rules that an alternative investment manager is not required to follow but instead they can choose to voluntanrily follow these rules. Voluntary compliance obligations can address compliance and operational matters that legislations and regulators completely ignore.

They can also address an area in which there is legislation and regulatory oversight; however, for a variety of reasons a fund manager has decided that more different and usually more rigorous compliance oversight is required. In this way, voluntary compliance often exceeds the minimum compliance requirements mandated by regulatory compliance obligations.

Regulatory Guidance

There are two categories of voluntary compliance obligations. The first category are those voluntary compliance guidelines that come from regulators. We will refer to these as *regulatory guidance*. Many times, financial regulators will provide recommendations with regards to practices they recommend an alternative investment manager could utilize in order to enact certain practices. In some cases, the practices in question are mandatory in nature and the regulatory guidance is merely encouraging a certain recommended approach by which the alternative investment fund manager could implement the mandatory obligation. In other cases, the practice is merely one that is encouraged by not mandated.

Regulatory guidance comes in many forms and from a variety of sources. One formal venue through which regulatory guidance can be communicated is through government testimony by regulators. Other less formal avenues through which regulators provide regulatory guidance can include through position papers and market commentary produced by regulators, by policy speeches and by regulators that are often given at alternative investment industry events or at universities. In recent years, regulators have become increasingly proactive in their efforts to communicate with the alternative investment community through educational events such as webinars and podcasts they host. Finally, in certain cases financial regulators may provide regulatory guidance through responses from questions on specific issues or market developments from legislative bodies or individual alternative investment firms.

Self-Imposed Obligations

The second category of voluntary compliance guidelines are those compliance obligations that an alternative investment firm places on itself. We will refer to these as *self-imposed compliance obligations*. These self-imposed obligations arise in two primary ways. The first way would be if a fund manager decides to adhere to the compliance guidelines that are not required by a regulator, but it wants to implement anyway. You may ask yourself why a manager would undertake such an additional compliance obligation on themselves, if it is not required? The answer is because a manager may have a desire to pursue industry's best practices that may go beyond the mandatory compliance minimums. Additionally, a fund manager may simply wish to have more frequent compliance oversight than would be minimally acceptable in already-mandatorily prescribed areas.

The second way that self-imposed compliance obligations can arise is when a fund manager commits themselves to follow the principles of third-party industry groups. Examples of such groups within the alternative investment space would be the CFA Institute, the Chartered Alternative Investment Analyst Association (CAIA) and the Institutional Limited Partner Association (ILPA).

Operational Compliance

With an understanding of the distinctions between mandatory and voluntary compliance, we can now turn our attention to another important compliance distinction, the difference between investment and operational compliance. *Investment compliance obligations* would be those directly related to activity in the alternative investment funds portfolio. An example of a mandatory investment obligation would be a private equity manager that purchases an equity stake in an olive oil manufacturer in Portugal. In this case, because of the specific relation of the investment to Portugal, the private equity fund would likely be subject to some oversight by the (Portuguese Securities Market Commission) known as the Comissão do Mercado de Valores Mobiliários (CMVM).

An example of a voluntary investment compliance obligation would be a hedge fund that has instituted a compliance policy that a single individual position in a fund cannot exceed greater than 15% of total fund assets. There is no regulatory rule that outlines this 15% limit, and it would be entirely self-imposed by the fund manager. It should be noted that just because a compliance obligation is self-imposed, as opposed to mandatory, does not mean that a fund manager can simply ignore the obligation once created. On the contrary, in most cases once the manager has documented that it will adhere to a certain policy, it must then follow it unless appropriate measures are taken to revise the compliance policy. A key reason for this is that investors are allocating capital to an alternative investment manager with an expectation that the manager will adhere to the policies they say they are going to, across many areas of the firm ranging from investment management through to compliance and operations. Investors undertake a great deal of effort to understand and analyze these policies during the operational due diligence process. For reference, this process is discussed in more detail in Chap. 10.

If the fund manager simply can change the policies and will have no obligation to document these changes and perhaps even pro-actively communicate these changes to investors, then most regulatory agencies have deemed that even though that the obligation was originally self-imposed, it effectively became mandatory for the manager once they implemented it upon themselves. This inherently makes sense, because otherwise a manager could promise investors that they would follow very robust compliance policies and then simply not expend the resource to implement them. When the fund managers' lack of effort was ultimately revealed, they could simply say that it was a change in policy but that no documentation was required. This would likely be a problem not only for regulators in most cases, as noted above, but also for many investors.

Operational compliance obligations refer to those compliance responsibilities that do not relate directly to the activities of the funds themselves but instead to the larger operation of the alternative investment firm. An example of a mandatory operational compliance obligation would be the requirement for US Securities and Exchange Commission (SEC)-registered firms to maintain books and records that support performance claims for at least five years under Rule 204-2 of the Investment Advisers Act of 1940. An example of a voluntary operational compliance obligation would be if a private equity fund manager determined that all employees should maintain record to be submitted to compliance of any gifts given or received to third parties in excess of $50. While there is general regulatory Financial Industry Regulatory Authority, Inc. (FINRA) guidance under FINRA Rule 3220 that a nominal value of a gift should not exceed $100, this guidance is not mandatory and many alternative investment firms in practice give and receive gifts well in excess of $100. Therefore, the $50 limit would be self-imposed on the fund by itself. Since the giving and receiving of gifts does not relate directly to the investment activities of a firm, therefore, this would be classified as an operational as opposed to compliance obligation.

It should also be noted that certain obligations related to both the investment and operational aspects of the firm; these can be referred to as *blended compliance obligations*. An example of such a blended obligation would be that a US Securities and Exchange Commission hedge fund manager that manages in excess of $100 million in certain covered securities would be required to file a specific form called a Form 13F within 45 days of the end of a calendar quarter that discloses a number of details regarding its holdings including their name, Committee of Uniform Securities Identification (CUSIP) number and total market value.[1] If an alternative investment manager does not breach this $100 million limit, then, according to this example, they would not need to file Form 13F. On the one hand, the filing of Form 13F is directly related to the amount of investment capital managed by the firm, and this could be classified as an investment compliance obligation. On the other hand, the amount of capital raised and managed by the firm, while influenced by investment performance, is also the result of non-investment-related efforts such as business development and client services. Therefore, the argument could be made that the filing of Form 13F could be an operational compliance obligation as well. Due to the dual investment and operational compliance obligations at play here, this could be classified as a blended compliance obligation.

Alternative Investment Governance Considerations

Traditionally, the term "governance" was applied in a corporate context. Notions of corporate governance refer to a rule-based framework to implement adherence to certain processes and procedures within a company. Historically, governance activist hedge funds often sought to unlock value at companies by promoting more effective governance structures. Often this was pursued in practice by fund managers seeking to nominate members of boards at underperforming companies.

In a broader alternative investment context, the term "governance" is a concept that is often related to notion of compliance management in alternative investment funds. From a compliance perspective, governance involves many of the same concepts as corporate governance, namely promoting effective controls. At alternative investment funds, a key mechanism of governance implementation has been boards of directors both at the individual fund level and asset management company level as well. In practice, governance is implemented at more than just the board level and is also put into place through the day-to-day activities of groups including risk management and compliance. Additionally, governance can be implemented through mechanisms such as firm-wide and departmental committee activities at the asset management company level. Governance in this broader sense can be defined as an interconnected system of controls and procedures that seek to promote independence, transparency and oversight through an alternative investment fund's ecosystem.[2] Governance and compliance are interrelated concepts that seek the promotion of adherence to rules to ensure the proper, efficient and compliance operation of fund managers. Approaching the concept of compliance, keeping in mind how governance operates in conjunction with it, is often a useful exercise to ensure that a fund manager is not overly focusing on one area at the expense of another.

Chief Compliance Officer Models

At alternative investment funds, the head of the compliance department generally maintains the title of chief compliance officer (CCO). In the majority of cases, CCOs are required to be designated by the regulatory environments of the vast majority of major jurisdictions in which alternative investment funds operate. For example, in the United Kingdom the Financial Conduct Authority (FCA) requires that FCA-covered firms designate a CCO in order to adhere to the rules of CF 10 compliance oversight function designation.[3] Similarly, in the United States, US SEC Rule 206(4)-7 of the Investment Advisers Act of 1940 requires that covered firms must maintain an individual that is designated as the CCO.

There are two primary types of CCO models employed. The first is what is known as an *in-house CCO model*. Under this model, the alternative investment fund employs resources from within the firm itself to fill the CCO role. In-house models can be further subdivided into two common approaches. The first is for the firm to utilize what is known as a *dedicated CCO*. This is an individual that is solely focused on the compliance function and does not maintain any other material non-compliance-related responsibilities. The second variation of the in-house CCO model is the *shared CCO model*. Under a shared structure, the CCO is not dedicated solely to compliance but has other primary duties as well. This framework is more common in smaller alternative investment funds that have less in-house resources to solely dedicate to compliance. An example of a shared CCO model would be an individual that serves as the chief financial officer (CFO) of a firm as well as a chief operating officer (COO) and CCO. Obviously, a dedicated CCO model is preferred from a compliance perspective because it allows an individual to focus solely on the compliance function rather than share their focus on other duties.

The second primary CCO model is an *outsourced CCO model*. Under an outsourced model, an alternative investment fund would have an individual that is not an employee of the firm itself, but instead an outsourced third party serves as CCO. This individual is a service provider referred to as a compliance consultant. For reference, the role of service providers is discussed in more detail in Chap. 5.

Chief Compliance Officer Duties

Regardless of whether the CCO is in-house or outsourced, in implementing the compliance function of an alternative investment firm a CCO must undertake certain duties. Similar to the framework for compliance obligations outlined earlier in this chapter, these CCO duties can be categorized into mandatory and voluntary ones. *Mandatory CCO compliance duties* are those tasks that are undertaken by the CCO to ensure that an alternative investment firm is adhering to its mandatory compliance obligations. An example of this would be ensuring that covered firms are indeed registered with the appropriate regulatory authorities and making regularly required filings with those regulators. *Voluntary CCO compliance duties* are those tasks that the CCO undertakes to facilitate voluntary compliance. This would include overseeing nonmandatory self-imposed restrictions in areas such as total bans on individual employees trading for their own securities accounts or receiving any gifts.

Common Compliance Documents

Fund compliance policies and procedures are often outlined in a variety of different fund documents. The core compliance document of most firms is something known as a *compliance manual*. In many cases, jurisdictions of financial regulators require that covered funds maintain a compliance manual. These manuals are often lengthy in nature and cover broad areas of basic compliance policies and procedures. Some of the items contained in this manual simply affirmatively state mandatory compliance obligations of the fund manager. For example, here is a sample section from a compliance manual of a US hedge fund that outlines that the fund must fill out a required form known as Form ADV:

a. The Adviser must complete and maintain an accurate Uniform Application for Investment Adviser Registration ("Form ADV"). The Adviser must complete Parts 1A, 2A (the "Firm Brochure") and 2B (the "Brochure Supplement," and together with the Firm Brochure, "Part 2") of Form ADV, as well as a series of Schedules thereto.
b. The Adviser is responsible for annually updating Form ADV within ninety (90) days of the end of its fiscal year ("Annual Updating Amendment"). The Adviser is also required to update its Firm Brochure (i) each year at the time it files its Annual Updating Amendment, and (ii) promptly whenever any information in the Firm Brochure becomes materially inaccurate.

The Brochure Supplement

a. A Brochure Supplement is required to be prepared for each Supervised Person who (i) formulates investment advice for a client and has direct client contact or (ii) makes discretionary investment decisions for client assets even if the person has no direct client contact.
b. While there is no obligation to file Brochure Supplements with the SEC, the Adviser is required to furnish the applicable Brochure Supplement to each of its advisory clients and prospective advisory clients before or at the time that a Supervised Person begins to provide advisory services to the client.

The information described in the section above is very technical and generic in nature and could effectively be applied to any alternative investment fund that is required to register with the US SEC and fill out Form ADV. This type of standard generic language is often referred to as being *boilerplate language*. Other information contained in the compliance manual may be more specific to the actual compliance policies employed at a particular fund. An example of this would be the following sample excerpt of personal trading and electronic communication surveillance:

Mary Smith, the CCO at ABCDEFG12345 Asset Management, LLC (or her designee) may use additional methods, such as electronic communications surveillance, to monitor for correlations between personal trading and noted conflicts of interest (such as board of director's service or personal relationships) and to identify potentially non-compliant activities or patterns between personal trading and fund manager trading. Additionally, all employees acknowledge that they will submit personal trades for pre-clearance through the firm's proprietary personal account dealing system.

You can see that the language above is more specific to the practices of a particular firm and are not mandatory but rather self-imposed in nature.

In addition to a compliance manual, an alternative investment firm may also prepare an accompanying document known as a *code of ethics*. This document is also sometimes referred to as a code of conduct and provides additional detail regarding the compliance policies employed by a firm. There is often overlap between the code of ethics and the compliance manual; however, the purpose of the code of ethics is to be more of a user-friendly document which employees can use to better understand and obtain more detail about day-to-day compliance practices as opposed to the more technically oriented compliance manual. Additional information regarding fund-level compliance specific is often located in the fund's offering materials and in particular in the *offering memorandum (OM)*, which is also referred to as a *private placement memorandum (PPM)*. An example of the type of compliance restrictions that would be specifically addressed to a particular fund in the PPM, as opposed to more firm-wide compliance concerns that would be outlined in the compliance manual, would be fund-level position limits in individual securities or regions.

Common Compliance Policies

Alternative investment funds maintains a wide variety of compliance policies and procedures. Many of these are rooted in mandatory compliance obligations that are then extended by firms into more rigorous self-imposed obligations.

Some compliance policies and procedures focus on the compliance aspects of information technology-related areas. These areas include data backup and archiving, cybersecurity, business continuity, and disaster recovery plan and telephone recording. For reference information technology operation considerations such as these are discussed in Chap. 6. Other common compliance policies include those in the following areas:

- Conflicts of Interest Policy
- Proxy Voting Policy and Guidelines
- Fair Credit Reporting Act
- Outside business activities
- Identity theft
- Environmental, social, and governance
- Custody policy and procedures
- Market Rumors Policy
- Gifts and Entertainment Policy
- Expense allocation
- Travel and expenses
- Political Donation and Activity Policy
- Valuation policies and procedures
- Anti-bribery policy and procedures
- Soliciting Prospective Investors Policy
- Privacy and Data Confidentiality Policy
- Whistleblower and anti-retaliation policy and procedures
- Personal Account Dealing Policy
- Pay to Play Policy
- Insider trading
- Monitoring of service provider and vendors

Chapter Summary

This chapter provided an overview of the compliance operations of alternative investment managers. It began with a discussion of the concept of mandatory compliance obligations. We next discussed the concept of voluntary compliance obligations. As part of this discussion, we outlined the sources of mandatory and voluntary compliance obligations. Next, we discussed the distinction between investment and operational compliance obligations. We then discussed chief compliance officer (CCO) models and the duties of CCOs. Other topics covered in this chapter include the role of governance in compliance management, compliance documentation including the compliance manual and code of ethics, and common compliance policies. In the next chapter, we will discuss the roles of service providers in alternative investment operations.

Notes

1. US Securities and Exchange Commission, Form 13F—Reports Filed by Institutional Investment Managers.
2. Scharfman, J., "Hedge Fund Governance: Evaluating Oversight, Independence and Conflicts," Academic Press, 2014.
3. Financial Conduct Authority, "Controlled functions,".

5

The Role of Service Providers in Alternative Investment Operations

Introduction to Alternative Investment Service Providers

Alternative investment firms, including hedge funds, private equity funds or fund of hedge all work with third parties in order to assist them in performing both their investment and operational functions. These third parties are vendors that sell goods or services to these funds. The term for the broad collection of these vendors is *service providers*. We have already introduced several service providers in our previous discussions in this book. These included administrators, prime brokers and executing brokers in relation to our discussion of trade operations in Chap. 2. Some service providers provide primarily fund-level services, while others provide services focused on the larger asset management company. Additionally, certain service providers may provide services at both levels. To continue our conversation of service providers in this chapter, we will first outline the broader role of the administrator in more detail outside of just the trade operations role it plays.

Fund Administrators

One of the most common alternative investment service providers is known as a *fund administrator*. Fund administrators provide a wide variety of services for funds. The work of fund administrator can generally be classified into two categories, fund accounting and shareholder services.

© The Author(s) 2020
J. Scharfman, *Alternative Investment Operations*,
https://doi.org/10.1007/978-3-030-46629-9_5

As a reminder we introduced the fund administrator in Chap. 2 in our discussion of the trade reconciliation process. The role of the administrator in the trading process relates to the accounting services they provide. It is important to note that an administrator often works in conjunction with the operations personnel in-house at an alternative investment fund manager. This is opposed to other services, such as law firms, that largely perform their services independent of the client (i.e. the fund manager). This distinction can be demonstrated, for example, in the area of trade capture. Common administrator services provided in this area would include the following:

- Handling the preprocessing of any trade files to facilitate the automated processing of any trades as applicable
- Setting up and maintaining securities in the administrators fund accounting system.
- Recording client-reported trading activity in the administrators portfolio accounting system

This could be compared with common fund manager responsibilities to the administrator with regards to trade capture:

- Providing the details of trade activities in a format previously agreed upon, which is usually done in an electronic manner
- Notifying the administrator prior to making any changes in the format or timing of trade files

Administrators often work in conjunction with other fund service providers as well. In a hedge fund context, an example of this would be an administrator receiving trade files from prime brokers as well as the fund manager to facilitate the reconciliation process.

Other common accounting services provided by administrators include the following:

- Calculation of profit and loss for funds
- Cash reconciliation services
- Calculate and verify interest and amortization accrual for fixed income instruments
- Process corporate actions to securities held in the portfolio
- Calculation of fees
- Calculation of the net asset value (NAV) of a fund
- Assisting with the preparation of fund statements and tax-related work

- Investment accounting
- Expense oversight including:

  - Accrue fixed expenses and organizational costs
  - Calculate and accrue fund expenses in accordance with the fund's offering memorandum
  - Allocate income and expense to each fund share class

- Partnership accounting
- Financial accounting and general ledger maintenance
- Performance measurement
- Other risk and portfolio-level reporting for fund managers and regulators
- Valuation assistance

Shareholder services refer to the tasks performed by the fund administrator with a focus on that information that relates to the investors in a fund. Common shareholder services performed by administrators include the following:

- Managing the process of receiving new capital subscriptions
- Managing the paying out of capital
- Performing anti-money laundering checks

Conflict of Interest Considerations

The administrator is commonly paid out of the expenses of the expenses of the funds to which it provides services. The money to cover these expenses comes from capital provided by investors in the fund. Therefore, in essence the investors are indirectly paying for the services of the fund administrator through a portion of their fund contributions. Investors do this because the administrator plays an important role in assisting the fund manager with operational duties. However, even though the administrator is paid by the fund, and therefore by the investors, ultimately the administrator in most instances based on the structure of funds often defers to the fund manager and not investors. This represents an inherent *conflict of interest* present in the fund administration relationship. While this conflict is common in the alternative investment space, investors should be aware of its presence and the specific ways in which the fund administrator may be carrying out their duties to place the interest of fund managers over that of investors.

Role in Valuation

Additionally, the administrator provides additional resources in the area of valuation oversight.

In regards to valuation in particular, it should be noted that hedge fund administrators do not usually maintain the authority to determine the final valuation of positions held by the fund. Rather, this ability to make a final determinative decision rests with the fund manager themselves. Similarly, the fund manager, not the administrator, generally maintains the final authority to approve the net asset valuation of a fund. These are important points and often one that causes some confusion for fund investors.

In practice, an administrator assists the fund manager in the securities valuation process not by calculating the prices of securities held by a fund themselves but instead by sourcing prices from independent pricing agents. In many cases, guidance on what types of third-party pricing agents are acceptable comes from a fund's offering memorandum. Additionally, a fund may also maintain a stand-alone pricing policy that provides further guidance in this regard. The purpose of the administrator with regards to valuation in this context is to serve as an independent aggregator of prices from a variety of third parties and then use these prices to calculate the fund's net asset value, which the fund manager must then approve.

At this point, you may be asking yourself, then what is the point of the administrator? After all, couldn't the manager simply source these prices themselves? The answer is yes, the manager could indeed source prices for securities themselves without the administrator. The role of the administrator is to serve as a third party that aggregates these prices. The theory is that if a third-party administrator is sourcing the prices and then using them to calculate NAV, there is some level of independent oversight in the process. Now of course, as we have outlined, the fund manager can override the administrator; however, the administrator also has the ability to resign from the engagement if they feel, for example, that the fund manager is incorrectly applying prices. In practice, the fund administrator often attempts to work with a fund manager to document and resolve any pricing differences between themselves and the fund manager in an amicable way.

It should also be noted that in some cases the administrator may not be able to source prices for all securities held by a fund manager. To understand situations in which this can occur, it is helpful to first understand a common grouping of securities utilized in the investment industry. In September 2006, a US organization called the Financial Accounting Standards Board (FASB) issued a *Statement of Financial Accounting (SFAS) 157*. For reference, in practice this statement was also historically referred to as FAS 157. More recently, FAS 157 became known under a new pronouncement called *ASC 820*. This statement provided a framework for measuring fair value under generally accepted accounting principles (GAAP). Specifically, ASC 820 / FAS 157 outlines three different levels across which securities can be grouped. Level 1 are the assets and liabilities which have the most transparent valuations. It is straightforward to obtain valuations for Level 1 instruments, and an example of such an instrument would be equity stock. Level 2 instruments are more difficult to value than Level 1, and often require indirect valuations. Often positions valued from broker quotes, rather than by observing direct equity prices, are Level 2 instruments. Level 3 positions are those for which the most unobservable levels of valuation inputs exist, and the data utilized for valuation purposes may not be able to be verified. Examples of Level 3 positions may include stock in privately held companies.

Returning to our discussion of the administrators role in sourcing inputs for the fund manager to approve the valuation, if no inputs are available, then the administrator cannot source them. As outlined above in the ASC 820/FAS 157 hierarchy, inputs are readily available for Level 1 positions and are available in most cases for Level 2 positions. Level 3 positions, in the vast majority of cases, are priced by the fund manager themselves. Another term for these types of positions is *manager marked positions*, because the fund manager is determining the valuation (i.e. mark) on their own. To be clear, this is not to imply that the fund manager simply picks whatever valuation they choose out of thin air. The manager often documents the assumption and reasoning that went into calculating their valuation including any third-party research or external support they utilized in determining the valuation. That being said, ultimately the valuation for Level 3 positions is in the managers discretion.

Valuation Consultants

Another type of service provider that an alternative investment fund may utilize is called a *valuation consultant*. These consultants often maintain specialized expertise utilized to value less liquid positions with few or a total lack of third-party observable valuation inputs such as Level 3 positions. In some cases, a fund manager may decide to work a third-party valuation consultant to assist them in determining the valuation of these positions. While hedge funds may utilize these consultants for less liquid positions in their portfolios, the use of third-party valuation consultants is more common in the alternative investment strategies that hold larger portions of their portfolio in illiquid positions such as private equity and venture capital.

It should be noted that simply because a fund manager maintains difficult-to-value positions in their portfolio, this does not mean that they will automatically engage a third-party valuation consultant to perform an independent valuation of a position. This is often at the discretion of the fund manager, subject to rules outlined in either the fund manager's private placement memorandum or another document known as a *valuation policy*. The cost of utilizing valuation consultants can be quite expensive, and, therefore, managers develop rules around their use, in part, to help keep costs down.

Valuation consultants typically provide three types of valuation services to fund managers. These services are provided typically after a fund manager has already attempted to value the position themselves. The first is what is known as *negative assurance*. This is the least detailed of the three valuation approaches, and often the cheapest. Under a negative assurance approach, the valuation consultant reviews the fund managers valuation policy as well as any specific pricing models the manager may have used in determining their own valuation to determine if they are reasonable in nature. The next level of valuation services is known as *positive assurance*. It builds upon the negative assurance to also have the valuation consultant review the specific inputs and methodology utilized by the fund manager in pricing the position. The last option is the most detailed and expensive one known as a *full valuation*. Under this approach, the valuation consultant develops their own pricing model and performs a detailed valuation of the position. The result of this can include a range of acceptable valuations or a specific value. Due to the high cost involved with this approach, it is not utilized very often in practice.

An example of the way a valuation policy rule regarding the use of valuation consultants may be applied in practice would be the following sample excerpt from a valuation policy:

> For position in excess of 10% of the fund, third-party valuations will be obtained on at least an annual basis. The fund manager will utilize a third-party valuation consultant from a pre-approved list of vendors.

In this example, positions greater than 10% are required to be valued at least annually. This 10% figure is completely up to the manager to determine. It could have been 15% or 30%. Or as noted above, the manager could have determined not to utilize a third-party valuation consultant at all and simply marked the position themselves. Often the decision to utilize a valuation consultant is made when the fund is first being structured and in conjunction with the initial large investors in the fund. Similar to the fund administrator, the use of these third-party valuation consultants provides investors with some degree of assurance that a third party is involved in the valuation process. Also similar to the structure employed for the fund administrator, the valuation provided by the valuation consultant is often not binding upon the fund manager. The fund manager could, therefore, disagree with the valuation provided by the consultant and utilize a different valuation.

Different valuation consultants often maintain different expertise with regards to hard-to-value assets and may apply different valuation approaches including the comparable approach and a variety of discount cash flow methods. In real estate, specific real estate model are utilized such as the income approach, the cost approach and the direct capitalization method by specialized valuation consultants called *appraisers*.

Compliance Consultant

A compliance consultant is an alternative investment fund service provider that provides compliance-related services to fund manager. As noted in Chap. 4, certain compliance consultants had historically even taken over the role of chief compliance officer (CCO) of a fund manager; however, this practice has largely been phased out and the CCO title is held in-house by an employee of the fund manager in most cases.

For newly launching fund managers, a compliance consultant may be engaged to assist the fund in preparing a regulatory compliance policies and procedures including a code of ethics and compliance manual. For more established fund managers, the compliance consultant can provide ongoing assistance regarding the operation of the compliance program.

Personal Trading Program Oversight

One of the common duties compliance consultants assist with is the oversight regarding a fund managers *personal trading program*. Also called *personal account dealing*, this refers to any trades that may be undertaken not by the funds that a firm manages but directly by employees themselves for their own personal accounts. It should be noted that in most cases personal account dealing compliance policies extend not only to fund managers' employees themselves but also their significant others and close relatives. Personal trading program compliance policies often require that employees submit trades for compliance, or the designated compliance consultant, for preapproval prior to proceeding with trade execution. In order to determine whether preapproval should be granted or not, fund managers often utilize a restricted list, which is a list that outlines securities that employees are prohibited from executing trades in. There are a variety of reasons why a security could be placed on the restricted list. One of the more common reasons is that the fund received material nonpublic information regarding a certain security, and, therefore, to prevent violations of insider trading rules, the fund manager banned employees from trading in this position.

Another common reason for a security being placed on the restricted list is because the funds that the firm manages currently hold a position in a security and they do not want employees trading in that specific security for their own account. The compliance consultant would cross-reference the submitted names for preapproval with the restricted list to determine if it was on the list or not. If it was not, then preapproval would be granted for the employee to trade. It should be noted that checking the restricted list is an example of only one personal account dealing compliance policy. There are often a host of compliance rules funds institute regarding personal account dealing that would have to be checked. These include the time frame during which an employee can institute a trade and restrictions regarding the frequency and volume of employee trades. In some cases, a fund manager or their compliance consultant may use automated tools to automatically perform checks regarding whether or not a particular employee trade would comply with the firm's personal trading rules.

Additionally, compliance checks are usually performed on a post-trade basis as well as by comparing brokerage statements from employee brokers with the trades submitted by employee for preapproval. This comparison process ensures that there were no trades that were executed but not submitted for approval by the employee. Depending on the number of employees and the volume of personal account dealing, the amount of work involved in successfully implementing a personal account dealing program can add up quickly. This is why increasingly fund managers are relying on automated tools and compliance consultants to assist with these types of resource-intensive compliance matters.

Electronic Communication Monitoring Oversight

Another common task that fund managers utilize compliance consultants for is to assist with what is known as *electronic communication monitoring*. Electronic communication includes methods of communicating such as email and instant messaging. Instant messaging is often utilized by traders and research analysts through a variety of popular platforms such as Bloomberg.

Fund manager archive and monitor electronic communications in order to ensure that employees are not violating the firm's compliance policies through inappropriate communications. The classic example of a violation would be an investor relations employee that tells a prospective investor that they guarantee a certain fund's investment performance in the future. A fund cannot guarantee performance since it cannot predict the future and, therefore, this is a violation of regulatory and compliance guidelines. Through electronic communication monitoring, searches for keywords commonly associated with violations, such as "guarantee," can be performed to detect and attempt to prevent future violations. In many cases, automated tools can be utilized to assist for monitoring for the use of certain specific keywords that are commonly associated with violations. Increasingly, electronic communication monitoring has begun to encompass social media reviews as well; however, this is a complicated area due to the privacy laws in different countries influencing employees' rights to post on social media. In summary, compliance consultants are often engaged to assist with electronic communication monitoring due to the time-intensive nature of this task.

Mock Audits

As with other service providers, it should be noted that the use of a compliance consultant is not mandatory, and some funds simply manage the compliance function entirely in-house. That being said, it is considered best practice for a fund manager to engage with some third parties, be they a law firm or compliance consultant, to provide a third-party evaluation of the firm's compliance capabilities with some regularity.

To accomplish this third-party evaluation goal, one task compliance consultants are often engaged by fund managers to perform is known as a *mock audit*. This a review of a fund manager from a compliance and regulatory perspective where the compliance consultant assumes the role of a financial regulator to which the fund is subject to review. The purpose of this review is to prepare a fund for an actual regulatory review. Oftentimes, mock audits can yield valuable insight to fund managers with regards to compliance deficiencies or potential deficiencies that can be corrected in advance of a real regulatory review. In order to simulate a real regulatory review, the mock audit process often includes the compliance consultant submitting a document request to the fund manager to complete, conducting on-site interviews with personnel and conducting random audits of the fund managers' implementation of compliance procedures.

Other Services

As the scope of alternative investment fund managers' compliance obligations has expanded, the tasks of compliance consultants are similarly expanding beyond the traditional realm of historical compliance duties. One primary example of this is the increasing number of service offerings by compliance consultants in the area of cybersecurity management and testing. Another example of that is in the area of business continuity and disaster recovery planning. A topic that has become increasingly important in the wake of extended business disruptions such as 2012's Hurricane Sandy and the 2019 Novel Coronavirus (COVID-19). For reference, the technology-related aspects of cybersecurity and business continuity planning are discussed in more detail in Chap. 6.

Other services commonly performed by compliance consultants include the following:

- Annual compliance reviews
- Trade surveillance
- Assisting in managing actually regulatory exams
- Compliance training
- Compliance surveillance and testing
- Vendor compliance reviews
- Expert network usage monitoring
- Regulatory reporting and filing
- Review of marketing and other investor facing materials
- Insights on industry happenings
- Regulatory compliant data hosting

Legal Counsel

Like most businesses, alternative investment fund managers utilize third-party law firms in a wide variety of ways. When a new fund is being launched, legal counsel is often utilized to assist the firm in setting up and registered the appropriate legal entities. Third-party law firms are also commonly utilized to assist in drafting the initial fund offering documentation including the private placement memorandum (PPM). Once a fund is up and running, law firms will often assist with revising existing fund documentation to reflect new organization or regulatory changes. These revisions are commonly reflected in separate documents called *supplements*. Law firms will also typically be called upon to assist with any litigation a firm may be engaged in ranging across a wide variety of issues from employee compensation disputes to investment related litigation dealing with a fund's investing activities. It should also be noted that depending on the structure of the funds involved and types of legal issues that are being dealt with in many cases, a fund manager may utilize several different law firms both domestically and abroad for different matters.

Increasingly, law firms and compliance consultants are offering overlapping services in competition from increasingly lucrative compliance and regulatory business for fund managers. As such, in recent years law firms now offer a wide variety of compliance-related services including drafting compliance manuals and related documentation, performing mock audits, employee training on compliance issues, ongoing compliance advice.

Accountants and Auditors

Third-party accounting firms often perform a number of services for fund managers. One of the most common services accountants are engaged for is to prepare the audited financial statements for the different funds managed by an alternative investment manager. These statements are typically prepared on an annual basis. In rare cases, to reduce fund expenses a fund manager may decide to hire an accounting firm to prepare audited financials for the fund not every year but for a longer period, such as every two or even three years. This is not considered best practice due to the lack of auditor oversight being extended for a period of greater than one year; but, while rare, such legacy arrangement still do exist, particularly among smaller private equity and venture capital funds. It should also be noted that similar to the use of other service providers it is not required that a fund manager hire an auditor in all cases.

In an even worse situation than spacing the audits out over several years, there are even rarer cases of small alternative investment fund managers that are still operating today that either prepare their own financial statements or work with an accountant, such as a certified public accountant (CPA) as they are called in the United States, to assist in preparing them but that do not produce fully audited financial statements. Once again, the typical motivation for doing this is motivated by costs concerns. It should be noted that while this decision is voluntary by the manager, the fund manager still has an obligation to investors to disclose in advance that they have opted to not have these financial statements prepared in an audited fashion or that they will be extending the period of the audit beyond the standard one-year time frame.

Other services third-party accounting firms commonly provide to alternative investment fund managers can include the following:

- Management company financial statement preparation
- A variety of tax advice and opinions related to the financial statements as well as potential investments
- Assistance in performing internal control and operational audits
- Auditing the fund manager for compliance with industry certifications such as Statement on Standards for Attestation Engagements (SSAE) 18 (formerly known as SAS 70 and SSAE 16)

Custodian

The role of a third-party service provider known as a custodian is to hold the assets of a fund. These assets can include both cash and securities. Custodians function in much the same way a bank does when it holds cash in escrow during the purchase of real estate, for example. In many cases, prime brokers will have related entities that serve as custodians for funds that they provide prime brokerage service to. It is important to note that when a custodian is holding the assets of a fund, it may do so in either the name of the fund or its own name. If a custodian does hold assets in its own name, this exposes the assets of the fund to greater counterparty risk should the custodian itself become insolvent and then the fund's assets could be exposed to recourse during the insolvency. Therefore, it is generally preferred that a custodian hold assets in the name of the fund as opposed to the name of the custodian.

Other Service Providers

In addition to the key service providers list above, alternative investment fund managers may work with a wide variety of other providers. Alternative investment fund managers are businesses, and in order to run their business from an operational perspective, they are required to interact with a great deal of third parties. Examples of these other service providers include the following:

- Real estate agents to secure office space
- Domestic and offshore banks to facilitate cash holding and movements for fund and management company activities
- Insurance brokers to assist in securing and maintaining insurance coverage
- Information technology consultants to assist in setting up and maintaining the firm's technology operations. For reference, these are discussed in more detail in Chap. 6.
- Human resources, payroll and benefits consultants
- Utility providers to provide common utilities such as telephones, electricity and heating and cooling services to physical office space

Chapter Summary

This chapter provided an overview of the different third-party service providers utilized by alternative investment firms. We began with an analysis of the role of fund administrators. As part of this discussion, we discussed the fund accounting and shareholder services they perform. We also outlined the inherent conflicts of interest present in the administration relationship, and the role of the administrator in the fund valuation process. We next discussed the role of third-party valuation consultants and the types of assurance services they offer. Next, we outlined the common duties of compliance consultants including assisting with personal trading program oversight and electronic communication monitoring. Finally, we discussed the role of legal counsel, auditors and other service providers that may be utilized. In the next chapter, we will discuss key aspects of the role of information technology in alternative investment operations.

6

Information Technology Operations

Introduction to the Role of Technology in Operations

As with most businesses in the modern era, information technology (IT) has played an increasingly important role in the day-to-day operations of alternative investment fund managers in recent years. The impact on technology can be seen on improving the efficiency of traditional fund operations in existing processes such as fund accounting or trade reconciliation. Information technology has also allowed funds to change the ways they do business through the use of automated trading algorithms and near-real-time risk management of investment risks. Increasingly, information technology has evolved to support the growing scope of complex compliance challenges facing alternative investment managers. As we outlined in Chap. 4, examples of this included the use of technology for ongoing compliance monitoring of electronic communications and for data archiving and regulatory reporting. In this chapter, we will focus on some of the more common operational processes in which information technology is utilized.

Information Security Policy

Increasingly, in order to maintain more consistent procedures and policies records from a compliance perspective, many alternative investment fund managers are documenting information technology policies as part of their

© The Author(s) 2020
J. Scharfman, *Alternative Investment Operations*,
https://doi.org/10.1007/978-3-030-46629-9_6

overall compliance program. A key focus of this documentation is in the area of information security. Many times, this information may be incorporated into the firm's compliance manual; however, in some cases a fund manager may develop a stand-alone *information security policy (ISP)*. These policies can cover a wide variety of topics including the following:

- Data protection, retention and disposal
- An overview of data access rights and the process by which employees can request to access restricted data
- Computer and laptop security protocols
- Login password requirements
- Software licensing and usage guidelines
- Data encryption standards and procedures
- Guidelines for the use of wireless networks

Similar to the way that many regulators require registered alternative investment asset managers to perform annual compliance training for employees, increasingly many firms are requiring employees to undergo mandatory information security training. This training is often provided for new employees during orientation as well as more formally throughout the year.

Information Technology Consultants

Within the alternative investment manager, the information technology function may be led by an individual with the title of chief technology officer (CTO). In some cases, a fund manager may not maintain an individual with the stand-alone CTO title but, instead, the duties of the CTO would be housed under an individual with another title with operational responsibilities encompassing the information technology function as well as other operational duties. Examples of such titles would be chief operating officer (COO) and chief financial officer (CFO). Depending on the size of the fund manager ,they may have a number of in-house staff focused on various aspects of information technology ranging from infrastructure and hardware to software development and support. As with most operational functions today, it is now common for a fund manager to utilize a combination of both in-house and external resources to support the information technology function.

Alternative investment managers utilize information technology consultants in a wide variety of capacities. Historically, many fund managers had a great deal of physical infrastructure hardware such as servers and networking equipment in their offices. Today, the bulk of alternative investment managers utilize information technology vendors' off-site cloud-based services, which has significantly reduced the need for this volume of equipment. This often includes a mix of both public and private cloud options to best balance the needs for security and data storage capacity while managing expenses for such services.

Once a fund has been established and is up and running, technology consultants also can provide ongoing services. These services include serving as a helpdesk in the event technology issues should arise and performing ongoing monitoring and maintenance of any on-site hardware in the fund managers' offices. In some cases, a fund manager may also seek to develop either a customized software to be incorporated into an existing application or a brand new piece of software to perform specific tasks.

While some fund manager do maintain software developers on staff, in many cases fund managers find it more efficient to outsource this work to third-party consultants. An example of this would be a fund manager that wishes to create a software that creates custom reports that can be utilized based on data from an off-the-shelf account system. Additionally, software developers may also perform ongoing updates and revisions to existing software. In many cases, a fund's information security policy will outline the firm's specific procedures by which software changes should be requested and initiated, testing should be done, and, finally, the new change should be implemented. In many cases, funds will utilize something called a *sandbox testing environment* to isolate the newly written code and test it before rolling it out to a live environment. The process and timing of the use of a sandbox would be an example of something that would be covered in the information security policy. Information technology consultants with specialized knowledge of certain systems may also be utilized to work on upgrades of enterprise wide systems. In the alternative investment space, this is often commonplace with complex legacy fund accounting systems.

Data Rooms

Increasingly fund managers utilize technology called *data rooms*. A data room is an Internet-based storehouse where information can be kept. Today, most data rooms are cloud based. The purpose of a data room is not only to facilitate the storage of historical fund data but also to assist funds in exchanging it with current and prospective investors. In many cases, a prospective investor will be directed by a fund manager to a data room in order to obtain a variety of pre-investment due diligence materials. On a post-investment basis, an investor may be directed to a data room to pull revised fund materials such as the latest fund risk reports. Information technology consultants often assist fund managers in selecting and utilizing data room solutions.

Cybersecurity

While the increased use of information technology among alternative investment managers provides many advantages, there are also a series of new and increased risks associated with its use. One of the biggest risks relates to the area of cybercrime. Cybersecurity can be defined as the risks associated with maintaining the integrity of an alternative investment manager's information technology infrastructure and data from unauthorized access of theft. When discussing cybersecurity, the first notion that comes to many people's minds are thoughts of clandestine hackers in remote countries launching virtual attacks again major companies to steal corporate intellectual property or individuals' credit card numbers. Alternative investment managers are also subject to cyberattacks. They make attractive targets to thieves for a variety of reasons including the wealth of intellectual property they maintain in the form of things such as proprietary trading algorithms, and the sensitive investor information and contact details that they maintain. Additionally, alternative investment managers are very sensitive to the negative effects of reputational damage to their firms that could occur in the event sensitive firm data were to leak and, therefore, might be good targets for cybercriminals to launch ransomware attacks on. A *ransomware attack* is a type of cyberattack where a hacker restricts a company's access to their own information and requires compensation, typically in the form of cash or virtual currency such as Bitcoin, in exchange for providing them access back or agreeing not to publish the information.

Penetration Testing

A penetration test is a way for an alternative investment manager to test for any weaknesses in an information security framework. In many cases, an alternative investment manager will hire a third-party technology consultant that specializes in penetration testing to perform the test. The manager may also perform their own penetration testing as well. The process of performing a penetration test is similar to a regulatory mock audit, except in this case the goal is to prevent cyberattacks as opposed to prepare for regulatory audits. The penetration testing exercise attempts to simulate the actions of someone with the goal of performing cybercrime. This could either be a third-party individual such as a hacker or be someone from within the firm such as an employee attempting to steal firm data.

Software Patches

Another key element of cybersecurity is ongoing software maintenance. In many cases, when a new version of a software program is released, it is to repair a vulnerability that had been uncovered in a previous version of the software. If a fund manager is slow to update the software with the latest update, often called a *patch*, then this vulnerability could be exploited.

A historical example of this was the 2017 WannaCry attack utilizing a specific type of ransomware attack called a *cryptoworm* to exploit unpatched software.[1] In the case of WannaCry and other cyberattacks such as the 2017 EternalBlue attack, a specific type of attack called Botnets was utilized. *Botnets* are networks of personal computers that are linked together in a clandestine way and then secretly controlled by the hacker to execute the cyberattack. In many cases, the patch process can be automated to pull new patches from software vendors once released. Despite this, automation manual oversight of the process is also recommended in order to ensure that the automated processes do not miss any critical patches. As part of this process, many information technology consultants perform ongoing patch supervision, which will prepare a patch report detailing what patches were updated as well as the date since the last patch of critical software applications. Therefore, it is important for either in-house or third-party information technology consultants to perform ongoing monitoring for software updates and patches.

Vendor Cybersecurity Analysis

As outlined in Chap. 5, alternative investment managers work with a wide variety of third-party service providers. These service providers maintain their own information technology infrastructures and are also subject to cybersecurity risks in the same way that the fund managers they provide services too are. Increasingly, before beginning a new relationship with a service provider, fund managers are devoting more efforts to analyzing the cybersecurity protocols in place at vendors. A large motivation for this is the increased regulatory scrutiny that has been placed in this area. Under regulations such as the European Union's General Data Protection Regulation (GDPR), fund managers can be held responsible for data breaches that take place at vendors under certain conditions. An example of how this would work in practice would be if a hedge fund manager works with a third-party administrator. If the administrator was subject to a data breach where the personal information of the hedge fund's investors was stolen, then under GDPR the hedge fund would have obligations to notify these investors of the breach and may also be exposed to financial penalties under the regulation. To be clear, in this example the hedge fund had nothing to do with the attack at the fund administrator, yet they still have obligations and potential liabilities because of it. Due to the potential for scenarios such as this, fund managers have developed a number of approaches to assess cybersecurity risks at vendors during the onboarding process. The specific steps taken by the fund manager in this regard often include the following:

- Sending the vendor a questionnaire to complete regarding their cybersecurity preparedness
- Conducting on-site or remote interviews with a vendor's in-house information technology personnel
- Evaluating the use of standard deterrence technology such as firewalls, analyzing the backup and storage of sensitive data
- Analyzing the use of any third-party information technology consultants
- Understanding if the vendor has a plan in place should a data breach occur

Business Continuity and Disaster Recovery

Business continuity planning and disaster recovery (BCP/DR) refers to the procedures and policies an alternative investment manager has in place in the event of a material business disruption. This business disruption can be temporary in nature or more long term. Examples of short-term business disruptions may include the temporary failure of Internet connectivity from a fund manager's office, a short-term power outage that causes a fund manager's office to lose electricity, and a small fire or a plumbing incident that causes employees to be out of the office for a day or two. Longer-term business disruptions are usually related to disaster-type events such as weather events like Hurricane Sandy and the 2019 Novel Coronavirus (COVID-19), which we referenced in Chap. 4.

Due to the vital nature of a fund manager being able to continue to manage investments and communicate with investors during times of crisis, BCP/DR planning has become increasingly an important part of a firm's operations. Oftentimes, the information technology function of an alternative asset manager is tasked with coordinating the implementation of BCP/DR plans. Oftentimes, in practice the work of the technology function in this regard is performing in coordination with other parts of the firm including the investment function and the compliance department. Many firms also develop a stand-alone business continuity and disaster recovery committee that is responsible for overseeing the implementation of BCP/DR plans. Compliance is also usually integral toward assisting the firm in developing a document known as a *business continuity and disaster recovery plan*.

Financial regulators are also increasingly requiring that alternative investment managers develop written BCP/DR plans. In the United States, the Securities and Exchange Commission (SEC), with regard to Rule 206(4)-7, outlines in part:

> We believe that an adviser's fiduciary obligation to its clients includes the obligation to take steps to protect the clients' interests from being placed at risk as a result of the adviser's inability to provide advisory services after, for example, a natural disaster or, in the case of some smaller firms, the death of the owner or key personnel. The clients of an adviser that is engaged in the active management of their assets would ordinarily be placed at risk if the adviser ceased operations.

Similarly, the National Futures Association (NFA) Compliance Rule 2-38 outlines that funds registered with the NFA are required to adopt business continuity and disaster recovery plans. Similarly, the UK's Financial Conduct Authority (FCA) Handbook in section SYSC 3.2.19 outlines that:

> A firm should have in place appropriate arrangements, having regard to the nature, scale and complexity of its business, to ensure that it can continue to function and meet its regulatory obligations in the event of an unforeseen interruption. These arrangements should be regularly updated and tested to ensure their effectiveness.

The development of a BCP/DR plan usually addresses a wide variety of aspects of a firm's plan for continued operation. One of the key areas that many asset managers plan for in the event of a business disruption is a way for employees to stay in touch and communicate when they cannot be physically present in the office. Plans in this regard often include instructions for employees to pass on information via email or through phone calling trees, alternative web portals that can be utilized to access the firm's systems remotely through virtually secure access, emergency contact details for employees, instructions for how to continue trading for approved employees from outside the office and instructions for how to use methods of communication such as video conferencing technologies. The following is an example of a sample language that would be contained in a BCP/DR plan with regards to a fund manager's communication plan in the event of a business disruption:

> The firm will communicate with employees via a communications tree. This tree includes several different means of communication including phone numbers (mobile and home) and individual employee personal email addresses. Additionally, in the event of a disruption, all firm staff will be required to attend a virtual conference call at 10:15 am, Monday through Friday. The information for this conference call is as follows:
> Participant Access Code: 55555
> Conference Dial-In Number: (555) 555-5555
> All employees have a listing of cellphone and home phone information electronically and in hard copy. Additionally, senior management each maintains a detail list of contact information for all material vendors in hard copy and electronic format at their residences.

Another item typically covered in BCP/DR plans is the designation of an alternative location from which employees may continue operations. This could include designating a formal location, known as a *disruption gathering location*. This is a location where employees would be directed to go in the event of a business disruption where the fund manager's office could not be accessed. The following is a sample excerpt from a BCP/DR plan with regards to the language that would commonly be seen in relation to a fund manager's office closure and remote working of employees:

> In the event of a significant business disruption that necessitates an office closure or evacuation, employees will utilize employee residences as alternate physical work locations. All employees either have desktop computers and/or laptops set up at home that are used for remote access. Currently each employee can access the firm's network (including all applications) from home via secure virtual private network (VPN).
> The firm has made the determination that mission critical business processes can all be supported effectively by a remote workforce with access to the Internet and telephony services. In the event of a significant long-term business disrup-

tion or outage of the firm's facilities, it will be the determination of the management as to whether or not the procurement of alternate physical workspace for use on either a temporary or long-term basis will be made.

BCP/DR plans also typically address the ways by which data will be archived so that in the event of a business disruption it would be accessible. Today it is considered best practice for fund managers in most situations to typically archive data on as close to real-time basis as possible. As noted above, in modern alternative investment fund managers the majority of data is stored off-site via the cloud; however, some firms may still use physical on-site backups as well for legacy reasons. In addition to data backup plans, BCP/DR plans will also typically detail the ways in which data can be accessed remotely in a secure way such as via a Secure Sockets Layer (SSL) connection.

Some of the other important considerations that should generally be addressed when evaluating what a BCP/DR should cover include the following:

• Are BCP/DR plans based on any industry certifications or guidelines?
• Are BCP/DR focused on a small list of specific events or do plans cover multiple scenarios?
• What does the plan cover in regards to outages of telephony and Internet loss?
• When a BCP/DR plan requires updating, who oversees updating the plans?
• Is separate office space maintained where employees could continue operations? If yes, how many seats are in such locations? If not, are employee expected to work from home?
• In the event that the fund manager has more than one office, what is the plan for employees from the different office to support each other to coordinate recovery efforts?

Earlier in this chapter, we discussed the role of information technology consultants and the cloud in supporting data archiving. The storage and access to data in the event of a BCP/DR event is another key consideration that is important to BCP/DR plans. Two key questions that should be considered when designing a BCP/DR plan with regards to data management are: How would employees be able to access data remotely and is this data storage and access secure? Another key consideration is the time frame involved in undergoing a data restoration. For example, if a disaster event occurs during the end of quarter when investor statements are due and it takes the hedge fund five days to perform a full data restore of their fund accounting system, this would likely cause a delay in the production of the fund manager's net asset value calculation and subsequent investor statements.

When a business disruption or a disaster event does occur, many funds then undergo a post-crisis evaluation to determine what lessons were learned from the event. In this way, the firm can determine what deficiencies may have been present in their current BCP/DR planning and how those weaknesses could be improved upon going forward. In many cases, failures of BCP/DR plan implementation come about not due to the failure of technology but rather due to human oversight.

A classic example of this is that of an alternative investment manager whose office becomes inaccessible due to a business disruption. The manager would have a robust BCP/DR plan in place. As part of this plan when such a business disruption were to occur, employees would work from home. The BCP/DR plan includes detailed instructions by which employees can securely access the firm's network under a work-from-home situation. The problem is that when an employee sits down to access the network, they realize they do not known their login password. Let us further assume that they do not have the phone number or email of the IT department or consultant, since it is stored on the computer. This failure of the BCP/DR plan, therefore, has nothing to do with the technology in place but is a result of simple human oversight. This example highlights the importance of not only drafting and implementing detailed BCP/DR plans, but also the need for testing these plans on a regular basis. When such tests are implemented, often issues such as an employee forgetting their login password become more apparent than merely by performing technology-based tests of plans. The following is sample language from an example of BCP/DR plan with regards to testing and plan updates:

> The fund manager anticipates that updates to the BCP/DR plans will take place whenever there are material changes to fund operations. Additionally, the BCP/DR committee will audit and review this plan on at least an annual basis for accuracy. Plan testing will be performed both in-house and by the firm's external information technology vendor. Formal testing will occur on at least an annual basis however, management recognizes the need and benefit for more frequent testing as well and will endeavor to do so at their discretion. Annual testing will include power and internet failover simulations as well as file server failure simulations. Training will also be conducted for each employee with regards to BCP/DR plans. Management will utilize the results of testing to improve BCP/DR planning at least annually. Additionally, on at least an annual basis employees will be required to attest that they have read and understand the firm's BCP/DR plans.

It should also be noted that similar to the vendor oversight of cybersecurity efforts, increasingly alternative investment managers are focused on the BCP/DR plans of their service providers. A key reason for this is that a disruption in the services provided by a key service provider, such as a prime broker, could directly impact the ability of the fund to successfully continue investment operations. Similarly, a business disruption at a service provider such as a fund administrator or auditor could impact a fund managers ability to distribute investor statements and audited financials in a timely manner.

Big Data in Alternative Investment Operations

The term *big data* refers to the process of using special computing applications to facilitate the analysis of very large sets of data in order to reveal trends and patterns. Alternative investment managers produce a great deal of data. Some of this data is stored and organized very accurately, such as data related to executed trades or the net asset value of a fund historically. Other types of data might not have been organized or even stored at all. An example of this would be the number of near-miss compliance violations with regards to a fund manager's gifts and entertainment policy, or the times a particular broker was unable to locate a bid for a particular security. Increasingly, fund managers are realizing that there is value in better tracking and organizing all of this data with a particular emphasis on fund operations.

A key motivator for this change in recent years has been increased pressure from financial regulators to better track and report on certain data such as fund risk exposures. Registered funds in the United States, for example, are also asked to calculate relatively newer metrics than they had in the past such as Regulatory Assets Under Management (RAUM). This calculation of these types of metrics requires access to more and better data. Additionally, investors in funds have increased the frequency and depth of their initial and ongoing operational due diligence requests. These requests have resulted in funds needing a better understanding of their data. It is also important to note that some funds have also incorporated the use of big data analytics as well as *artificial intelligence*–related solutions to big data problems on the investment side of their business as well. These efforts have also resulted in more insights with regards to areas such as identifying potential compliance challenges on the investment side with more lead time as well as more insightful risk management strategies.

Chapter Summary

This chapter discussed the role of technology in alternative investment manager operations. The chapter began by outlining the role and items typically covered in information security policies. Next, we discussed the role of information technology consultants and the range of duties they typically perform for fund managers. As part of this conversation we discussed the software development life cycle including the process for change management and sandbox testing. We then discussed the role of data rooms in archiving and distributing management company and fund information. Next, we outlined cybersecurity trends with regards to fund operations including the role of penetration testing, software patches and vendor cybersecurity analysis. We concluded the chapter with a discussion of business continuity and disaster recovery planning and the role of big data and artificial intelligence in alternative investment operations. In the next chapter, we will discuss a variety of other additional functions and tasks that are important to fund operations.

Note

1. *See* M. Bowden, "The Worm That Nearly Ate the Internet," *The New York Times*, June 29, 2019

7

Additional Operational Functions and Tasks

Introduction to Additional Operational Functions

Up until this point in the text, we have provided an overview of a some of the most important operational areas within alternative investment funds. In practice, there are a wide variety of different operational areas that function within an alternative investment fund manager. In this chapter, we will provide an overview of these other areas beginning with an overview of operational risk management approaches.

Operational Risk Management

Operational risk can be broadly defined as, "the risk of loss resulting from inadequate or failed internal processes, people and systems, or from external events."[1] Practically, operational risk at alternative investment fund managers encompasses the process and procedural risks associated with the non-investment activity of a fund manager. This can be distinguished from investment risk management which relates directly to the investment activities of a fund. For example, the risks associated with the ability of a fund to continue operations in the event of a power failure would be operational risk. The risks associated with losing millions of dollars in a portfolio because of an incorrect decision to be overexposed to the commodities would be investment risk.

© The Author(s) 2020
J. Scharfman, *Alternative Investment Operations*,
https://doi.org/10.1007/978-3-030-46629-9_7

The concept of *operational risk management* (ORM) refers to analyzing and managing the operational risks at a fund. For the purposes of this text, we will use the term "ORM" to refer to operational risk management undertaken by firm management within the firm itself. This will be distinguished from the term "operational due diligence" (ODD), which refers to the external review process undertaken by prospective and existing fund investors in order to evaluate the operational risk framework within a fund manager. For reference, the operational due diligence process is discussed in more detail in Chap. 10.

Fund Reporting

Alternative investment fund manager reporting has become increasingly sophisticated in recent years. A key driver of this fact is that fund managers have made increased use of information technology integrated with better data science tools. This has allowed fund managers to track and report their data more efficiently and effectively. Along the same lines, fund administrators, who also provide reporting to investors through their shareholder services capabilities, have similarly increased the quality of their service offerings. Historically, when meeting with prospective investors, a marketing presentation would be prepared, which would include a variety of operational and investment data including background information about a fund's background, historical investment performance, investment professionals, information about the funds being considered for investment and their future investment opportunities. This presentation is commonly referred to as a *pitchbook*.

In recent years, alternative investment fund managers, and hedge fund managers in particular, have sought to increase the level of communication with prospective investors. Part of this increased communication has been driven by regulatory changes that have loosened the marketing restrictions on alternative investment fund managers. An example of this, in the United States, is the 2012 Jumpstart Our Business Startups Act, also known as the JOBS Act. Under this legislation, and subsequent Securities and Exchange Commission (SEC) –related action, fund managers were able to increase their marketing outreach to investors, particularly those in the retail space.

As part of this trend of better communications and increased outreach, many hedge funds prepare what are known as *tearsheets*. Tearsheets are short summaries of fund performance and other relevant information during a particular period of time. Tearsheets may be prepared for a specific fund vehicle or fund strategy. Typically, tearsheets also contain background information about the fund manager as well. Some funds distribute tearsheets on a monthly basis, while others may do so less frequently, such as on a quarterly basis. Tearsheets may also be distributed to both existing and prospective fund investors. Tearsheets usually begin by including a summary of the investment objective of the fund. Tearsheets also typically include a summary of investment data such as guidelines regarding current fund holdings, a fund performance history and a comparison of fund performance to a benchmark. Increasingly, tearsheets contain updates on fund operational data as well including the following:

- Current number of employees
- Details regarding firm, fund and strategy assets under management
- Summary of key service providers and counterparties
- Background information on a fund or strategy including launch dates and key personnel
- Summary of fund terms including fees, high water marks, redemption frequency and notice period, redemption gates

Human Resources Management

An alternative investment fund manager, just like any business with employees has a variety of human resources considerations. The human resources function at a fund manager typically includes activities such as new employee recruitment and hiring, benefits management, payroll processing, dealing with employee complaints in areas such as harassment or workplace disputes, terminating employees, communicating relevant human resources updates to employees and providing ongoing training on human resources policies and procedures.

As with most operational function at fund managers today, the duties of the human resources function are typically performed through a combination of in-house and third-party service provider resources. Third-party human resource vendors in this space come in a variety of forms. Some offer a wide array of human resource–related services, while others specialize in certain areas such as payroll processing or benefits management. Whether the process is outsourced entirely to a vendor or not, compliance and operational personnel at a fund manager are typically involved in some aspects of the day-to-day management of human resources to oversee the work of the vendor.

Security Master Files

In order to value securities, fund managers must look to either third-party valuation inputs or internal valuation models resulting in manager marks. As discussed in Chap. 10, fund managers work in conjunction with third parties called administrators to assist them in providing oversight in sourcing valuations as well. During the valuation process, increasingly it is up to the operations department, often with guidance from the investment team, to ensure the proper sourcing of valuation inputs. For securities, such as publicly traded equities, today this is often an automated process that involves the fund managers fund accounting and trading systems automatically pulling pricing data from exchanges and data vendors. For less liquid position, the process often involves the operations professionals sourcing valuations from third-party brokers. While investment personnel may lead this process due to their ongoing dialogues with brokers for trading purposes, it is often up to operations to coordinate the gathering and processing of this data.

This is an important point to note, particularly in regards to valuations. The role of operations is to facilitate the work of the investment side of an alternative investment manager's business, but this does not mean that the investment team proceeds howsoever it would like, and it is left to operations to clean up the pieces. On the contrary, the operations and investment functions must work hand in hand to ensure proper processing and accounting for the investment activities of the firm. One example of this that relates to both trading and valuations is a concept known as the *security master file*. A security master file is a computer file that serves as a repository for relevant data about the securities that are being traded by a firm. It can be thought of as a menu of trading options that operationally available to traders. The term "operationally available" is used here because the securities listed on the security master file are those that have already been set up in the firm's systems. If a particular security is not listed in the security master file, it does not mean that a trader cannot execute a trade in the position. On the contrary, it simply means that an entry for the security, along with its relevant details have not yet been created in the firm's security master file repository.

Security master files contain a wide variety of descriptive information about securities. This information typically includes a number of background data points about the security depending on the type of instruments being traded including the following:

- Issuing company name
- Ticker symbol of the security
- Security type (i.e. common stock, preferred stock, warrant, bond etc.)
- Primary market the security is traded in
- Any secondary or other markets the security is traded in
- Designation of market makers in the security
- Minimum price variations (MPV) for the security
- Shares outstanding
- ISO 4217 currency and country codes
- Classification of financial instruments (CFI) code
- Relevant state codes
- Debt features including closing date, first coupon date, interest payment frequency, tender agent, rate type and secondary insured

Unique Identifiers: CUSIP and ISIN

The security master file also typically contains a unique identification number. In North America, this identification number is commonly known as a Committee of Uniform Securities Identification (CUSIP) number. A *CUSIP number* is nine characters in lengths. These nine characters are broken up into groups. The first six characters help identify specific information related to the company, municipality or agency issuing the security. The next two characters (i.e. numbers four and five) outline the type of security in question such as equity or debt. The final digit is used to check the accuracy of the previous eight digits. For example, the CUSIP for Amazon.com Inc common stock is 023135106, where 023135 identifies the company, 10 identifies the instrument type (i.e. common stock) and 6 is the mathematical check figure.[2]

For other securities that are traded internationally, in many cases they will maintain not a CUSIP but a unique identifier known as an *International Securities Identification Number (ISIN)*. ISINs are 12-digit numbers. The first two characters describe the country where the security is from, the proceeding nine numbers then identify the region, issues and type of instrument. Similar to the CUSIP, the final number is a check number to verify accuracy of the previous numbers. CUSIP numbers and ISIN numbers may be relatively similar. For comparison, ISIN of Amazon is US0231351067, which is the same as the CUSIP number with some additional verifying information included to adhere to the ISIN format. Security master files may also contain other types of unique identifiers depending on the type of securities being traded. An example of this would be a Central Index Key, which is a number utilized for SEC filings purposes, and a Stock Exchange Daily Official List number (SEDOL), which is typically utilized for UK and Irish securities.

Multiple Versus Universal Security Master Files

Earlier in this discussion we referenced that operations sets up a security in the security master file but we didn't go into detail as to what this process entails. Typically, the process entails logging a wide variety of information about each security. A key problem related to the use of security master files historically is that certain systems utilized different security master files. This resulted in situations where different copies of security master files were in place with potentially different types and amount of identifying information about the same security. This often led to confusion and errors in consolidating the data after it was processed through different systems with each respective security master file. To correct this problem and promote consistency, it is preferred where possible to utilize a *universal security master file*, which allows for a single consolidated source for all identifying security-level information that can be utilized by all systems. This universal file is sometimes referred to as the *prime copy* or *golden copy* of the files.

File Verification Sources

Another consideration with regards to the setup of a security in the security master file is the independent verification of a securities characteristics once they have been loaded in by operations. Historically, managers may have utilized only a single source to verify this information. The problem with this approach of a single-source verification is that with only one source there is a lack of corroboration among multiple parties and this could lead to errors. This is why multiple sources of verification are preferred for security master files. The independent verification of the security master file can come from a variety of third-party data vendors.

As with most operational procedures, there is a trend that the setting up of a new security and subsequent independent verification of the accuracy of security master file data is increasingly automated. This is generally considered to be more efficient and less prone to manual error. This does not mean that

the operations department should not be involved in the assisting with estab-
lishing the automated procedures involved. Additionally, it is considered best
practice for a fund manager's operations department to be involved in auditing the quality of the security master file's automated setup, verification and
updates on a rolling basis. Operations also typically takes the lead in communicating the updating and maintenance of the security master file with the
investment function to ensure that any new securities that may be potentially
traded by the firm's funds are accurately loaded into the security master file so
that they may be traded and accounted for efficiently at the discretion of the
investment team.

Trading and Valuation Implications

The concept of the security master file is important because, ideally, the investment side of a fund manager should give notice to the operations function
with regards to what types of securities they wish to trade. This allows the
operations team to then code the security-specific details into the firm's systems so that they are set up to appropriately handle and track all the relevant
operational procedures that could be associated with a security from new
trades and purchases of the security to the eventual sale of the security. The
information contained in the security master file not only drives this trading
process but has longer-term implications for the life of the security within the
fund manager because the characteristics of a security loaded in the security
master file also impact its identification and use for processes further down
the operational pipeline such as valuation.

The way this works in practice is that an investment professional at a fund
manager would decide that they would like to trade in a particular type of
security or market. If this is a relatively straightforward extension of trading
activities, then it is likely that the security master file already contains the
appropriate security detail because it has been preloaded from a data vendor.
The data vendors security master set usually contains millions of security types
that may be listed as well as over-the-counter (OTC) positions. For example,
if the fund manager has typically traded a certain list of companies public
equity and now decides to start trading in new public equities, the entries for
this public common stock is likely already in the security master file. If, however, the fund manager decides to start trading in more exotic instruments or
in new global markets, then these securities may not already be listed in the

security master. It is examples like this under which the investment manager would do well to communicate with operations personnel so that they can set up the new securities in the security master file prior to trades being executed.

When the trade is executed and then after a trade is complete, the firm's various trading, back office and accounting systems pull the security data from the security master file. Under a university security master file approach, they are all accessing the same data from the same file, as opposed to different databases. If this information is not accurate, the errors would then be compounded across multiple systems. This is why it is important for the operations department to ensure that the information in the security master file is accurate and validated on an ongoing basis.

Insurance

Alternative investment fund managers, like most other businesses, commonly maintain a variety of different types of insurance coverages. Some of this insurance relates to the day-to-day management of the asset manager's business at the firm-wide level. Other types of insurance relate to fund-level insurance. In certain specific cases, a fund manager may be required by an investor or regulator to maintain specific types and amounts of insurance. An example of this would be an investor that falls under the Employee Retirement Income Security Act of 1974 (ERISA) requiring that a fund manager maintain a type of insurance known as an ERISA bond in order to manage capital for them. Another example would be requirements put in place by different US states that employers, including asset managers, maintain unemployment insurance or workers compensation insurance. Outside of these special types of situations there are generally no specific requirements with regards to the amount and type of insurance coverage that a fund manager must maintain. That being said, there are a number of more common types of insurance that a fund manager will maintain.

A key question many fund managers must evaluate when securing insurance is what the coverage amounts and deductibles should be. Many managers rely on a third-party service provider called an *insurance broker* to assist in determining what kind of coverage to specifically obtain as well as for guidance on the amount of coverage for each type of insurance obtained. It should also be noted that some fund managers have opted to not obtain third-party insurance for certain risks but to *self-insure*. Under a self-insurance approach, the fund manager weighs the costs of obtaining third-party insurance versus the risks of directly covering the financial losses from that risk. For certain types of coverage, depending on the size of the fund manager, typically some combination of self-insurance complemented by third-party insurance seems to be a compromise approach that most alternative investment fund managers have taken.

Key person insurance refers to the insurance maintained by a firm on what are deemed to be essential personnel. This insurance provides financial compensation to the fund manager in the event a key person cannot perform their duties with regards to the funds. A chief investment officer is an example of an individual on which key person insurance could be typically maintained. There are many variations with regards to the specific types of key person insurance that can be maintained. For example, do they cover situations in which the fund manager may be temporarily incapacitated, such as an illness, or would a longer-term lack of involvement be required. Key person insurance could also get into more exotic area of coverage such as insurance in the event a key executive of the firm is kidnapped. This type of ransom coverage gained attention in the alternative investment space when a fund manager of an investment manager from ESL Investments named Edward Lampert was kidnapped while leaving his office and held at gunpoint for almost two days before convincing the kidnappers to let him go. With ransom insurance coverage in this situation, the losses, and potential ransom money, may have been covered entirely or in part by the insurance policy.

Another type of insurance that fund managers are increasingly securing is cybersecurity insurance. This insurance would provide coverage in the event of losses due to damages from cybercrime. Once again, there are many varieties of cybersecurity insurance that include everything from recovery due to data breaches to business disruptions due to cybercrime.

Two common related type of insurance policies include those for what is known as errors and omission (E&O) and directors' and officers' liability (D&O) coverage. Other types of coverage may include employment practices liability coverage and management company and general partner liability.

Treasury Function

Increasingly, over the past several years many alternative investment funds, and particularly hedge funds, have established stand-alone treasury functions within their organizations. While the specific tasks of the treasury function vary in relation to the different investment strategies employed by managers, the key tasks usually performed by treasury functions include counterparty management, portfolio financing, cash and collateral and margin management.

Portfolio Financing

The portfolio financing role of the treasury department consists of centralizing the financing process to facilitate trading. This financing includes borrowing cash and stock on margin to facilitate trading. When cash is moved to facilitate trading in this way, it falls into the cash utilized for trading category referenced earlier in this chapter. When this financing function is not centralized, it is often left to the fund's individual traders to negotiate financing including rates and associated pricing. Increasingly, hedge funds are utilizing automation to be more proactive with regards to the rates earned from stock-lending positions, which can increase the savings earned through tighter ranges for difficult to borrow positions and overall better pricing.[3]

Counterparty Management

In the broadest sense, counterparties can refer to any vendor that a fund has exposure to. This can be exposure through avenues including reputational risk, operational risk or financial risk. In the context of the treasury function, counterparties are commonly referred to as being institutions that are involved in the trading process. This could include other parties to trades, as well as intermediaries such as prime brokers. Increasingly, treasury functions as focusing more heavily on the oversight of counterparty broker reviews across a variety of areas including their ability to supply capacity for shorts and hard-to-borrow securities, the rates being charged to funds for executing trades and the overall quality and speed of their execution.

Collateral and Margin Management

Collateral and margin management involves overseeing the assets that have been pledged by one party to another for the purpose of reducing the credit risk between the two parties in the event of a default. Increasingly, funds have centralized the collateral and margin management process in the treasury function in order to provide more systematic oversight of the process.

In addition funds have transitioned towards centralized process because it better facilitates operational efficiencies to deal with increasingly complex challenges. An example of this would be the increased use of more complex loans arrangements such as *cross-collateralization*, where one loan is utilized as collateral for another loan. The collateral and margin management process is also increasingly highly regulated and can require funds to monitor and document a wide variety of risk, legal and regulatory data. As such, increasingly funds are not only centralizing the collateral and margin management processes in the treasury function but are also utilizing specialized systems to assist with this process including performing calculations for margin calls. It is also important to note that the collateral management process involves a fund having exposure to counterparties, and, as such, centralizing both the collateral and margin management process and counterparty management process in the treasury function makes sense.

Chapter Summary

This chapter provided an overview on the wide variety of operational functions present at alternative investment managers. We began with a discussion of operational risk management and fund reporting. We then discussed important fund manager operational policies for human resources management. Next we discussed security master files. As part of this conversation, we discussed the concepts of unique identifiers for securities within files including CUSIP and ISIN numbers. We then discussed operational considerations for fund manager insurance management. Finally, we concluded with a discussion of the treasury function. In the next chapter, we will discuss unique considerations for private equity operations.

Notes

1. Basel II: International Convergence of Capital Measurement and Capital Standards: A Revised Framework," June 2004.
2. See CUSIP Global Services, "Structure of a CUSIP" (n.d.)
3. See Euromoney Seminars, "Hedge Fund Treasury Units Taking On Greater Role" (n.d.)

8

Private Equity Operations

Introduction to Private Equity Operations

Private equity funds are a category of alternative investment managers that traditionally invest capital into more illiquid holdings of companies. There are a broad range of types and styles of private equity funds ranging from early-stage venture capital funds to later-stage private equity investors. Additionally, the amount of capital invested by different types of private equity funds can vary greatly. As a result of the types of investments made by private equity funds, they have certain unique operational aspects in place. This is in comparison to other types of alternative investment managers such as hedge funds that traditionally invest in more liquid types of instruments that trade more regularly.

From a structural perspective, many private equity firms maintain commensurate operational resources and structures to their alternative investment counterparts. Therefore, it would not be uncommon to see individuals with many of the same operational titles one would come across at other alternative investment managers. These titles could include chief operating officer (COO), chief compliance officer (COO), chief technology officer (CTO) and chief financial officer (CFO). The specific operational duties performed, however, would be applied as applicable to private equity versus other alternative investment managers. In this chapter, we will discuss some of the more important private equity specific considerations.

© The Author(s) 2020
J. Scharfman, *Alternative Investment Operations*,
https://doi.org/10.1007/978-3-030-46629-9_8

Private Equity Structure

To begin our conversation in this chapter, it is useful to clarify some specific private equity terminology.

- Portfolio company—Not all private equity firms invest into companies but for those that do, the term "portfolio company" or underlying company is used to represent the company that a private equity company would make an investment in.
- Limited partner—This is an investor in a private equity fund. Most private equity funds, in addition to hedge funds, are organized under a legal structure known as a limited partnership, and therefore the investors in this structure are referred to as limited partners (LPs)
- Private equity manager—Also referred to as a private equity manager, is the management entity responsible for managing the private equity company itself.
- General partner—A private equity firm and funds are effectively overseen by an entity known as general partner (GP) of the funds.

It should be noted that in practice there is often a legal distinction drawn between the private equity firm and GP but in practice the term "GP" and private equity manager may be utilized synonymously.

Private Equity Administration

In Chap. 5, we discussed the role of a fund service provider known as a *fund administrator*. As a reminder, fund administrators offer a variety of services that can be grouped into the two primary categories of shareholder services and fund accounting services.

In the early days of the hedge fund industry, the use of third-party administrators was quite uncommon. During that time, a hedge fund would perform all the traditional administrator service in-house. This is referred to as a *self-administration model*. Over time as investors and fund managers became more sophisticated in their demands for both operational efficiencies and independent oversight, there was a growth in the use of third-party administrators. Today, the use of administrators in the hedge fund space is extremely commonplace. So much so that most institutional investors would not invest in a hedge fund that was self-administered.

As compared to their hedge fund counterparts, many private equity managers still adhere to a self-administration model. One common reason often cited for the reluctance of investors to insist on private equity administration is because of the focus on the administrators role in the valuation oversight process. Private equity funds typically invest in privately held and less liquid investments. Recalling the FAS 157 / ASC 820 valuation grouping framework we discussed in Chap. 5, private equity investments would generally be classified as Level 3 positions, that is, those for which the most unobservable levels of valuation inputs exist. This is in contrast to hedge funds which largely hold more liquid Level 1 and Level 2 instruments. For hedge fund Level 1 positions, the administrator can source valuation inputs from a wide variety of sources. Even for Level 2 positions, which are less liquid, there are usually several sources such as a variety of broker quotes available. For Level 3, no such quotes are generally available. As such, the question becomes, what benefit can a third-party administrator provide with regards to private equity valuation oversight? Because of this question, many private equity general partners have historically not felt the same pressure their hedge fund counterparts have to engage third-party administration services for their funds and have instead opted to self-administer.

One response to this question of the value of third-party administrative oversight with regards to the valuation process relates not to the specific values attributed to positions but the overall GP valuation process employed. For example, consider a private equity manager that has a fund that invests $30 million for a 25% stake in an underlying portfolio company in the healthcare space. Now let's fast-forward one year in the future, what is the value of this original $30 million investment today? A fund administrator would also not be able to find a third-party independent valuation source that can provide this value in the same way they can look up the value of a share of Facebook stock from a vendor such as Bloomberg or Reuters. Similarly, a fund administrator would not be expected to independently calculate the value of this position on their own the way a different vendor known as a *valuation consultant* would. What the administrator could do is to provide some level of oversight to ensure that the fund manager is adhering to their own valuation policies with regards to performing their own in-house valuations.

For example, a GP's valuation policies could outline that they are expected to perform a valuation of each position on a quarterly basis. As part of this process, the GP would typically produce a valuation memorandum summarizing what they feel the current valuation of the position should be as well as any supporting documentation and models that provide support to this manager mark. If a GP self-administers their own funds, outside of ongoing due diligence follow-ups, it is up to investors to trust that the GP is producing these memos. With the presence of a third-party administrator, the administrator would typically require that the fund manager share these memos and that the administrator would retain a copy of them. If the GP doesn't send the administrator a memo in a certain quarter, the administrator would then follow up and remind the manager of their obligation to do so under the valuation policies. This is assuming of course that the fund administrator has been engaged to provide this level of oversight. The specific scope of services provided by an administrator to a fund are uniquely negotiated for each individual engagement.

Increasingly, many private equity firms are transitioning to utilizing third-party administrators. As outlined in the valuation oversight example above however, they are typically utilized in different ways than the traditional administration model employed for hedge funds. The common services provided by private equity fund administrators include the following:

- Maintaining books and records of administered funds for accounting purposes
- Reconciling cash movements to relevant fund bank accounts
- Processing capital calls and capital distributions
- Assistance in overseeing cash movements and disbursements
- Calculations of hurdle rates, preferred return, management fees and carried interest
- Fee waterfall calculations and subsequent allocations
- Performance reporting
- Know your customer (KYC) and anti-money laundering (AML) checks
- Compliance assistance including data compilation and filing with regulations such as the Foreign Account Tax Compliance Act (FATCA) and Securities and Exchange Commission (SEC) forms including Form ADV and Form PF
- Management company accounting and budgeting
- Limited partner reporting

Private Equity Valuation Policy Example

While the administrator may play a more limited role in the private equity valuation process, this is not to say that private equity firms may not have some exposure in their portfolios to limited quantities or more liquid assets.

The reasons for this could include foreign exchange exposure due to currency hedging or small positions in more liquid equities and debt from, for example, a smaller post-IPO position in a portfolio company. As such, private equity valuation policies will still typically address instances of not just Level 3 position but also Levels 1 and 2. To demonstrate how this is implemented in practice, we have included the following example private equity valuation policy:

The general partner ("GP," or the "Firm") has established and adopted this valuation policy and procedures manual to adhere to the rigorous financial reporting requirements under Financial Accounting Standards Board ("FASB") Accounting Standards Codification Topic 820, Fair Value Measurements and Disclosures ("ASC 820"), formerly known as FAS 157. This policy was additionally established to comply with requirements applicable to it as a Registered Investment Adviser under the Investment Advisers Act of 1940 ("Advisers Act").

Fair value is generally defined in ASC 820 as the amount at which an investment could be exchanged in a current transaction between willing parties, other than in a forced or liquidation sale. The objective is to estimate the exchange price at which hypothetical willing marketplace participants would agree to transact. The Firm will seek to have consistency in its valuation methodology with respect to a portfolio company over time, as applicable. Fair value is based on the assumptions market participants would use when pricing the asset or liability. In support of this principle, the Firm utilizes a fair value hierarchy as promoted by generally accepted accounting principles ("GAAP"). These principles emphasize the information used to develop those assumptions. Capitalized terms used but not otherwise defined herein have the meanings ascribed to them in GP's Compliance Manual. ASC 820's recommended hierarchy of valuation metrics is summarized below:

- Level 1: Quoted prices in active markets for identical assets or liabilities;
- Level 2: Observable inputs other than quoted prices, such as the following:

  - a. Level 2a: Quoted prices for similar assets or liabilities in active markets;
  - b. Level 2b: Quoted prices for identical or similar assets or liabilities in markets that are not active;
  - c. Level 2c: Inputs other than quoted prices that are observable for the asset or liability (such as interest rates, yield curves, implied volatilities and credit spreads);
  - d. Level 2d: Inputs derived from or corroborated by observable market data by correlation or other means

- Level 3: Unobservable inputs for the asset or liability.

Methodology

GP values its investments on a quarterly basis in accordance with the fund's limited partnership agreement. Additionally, valuations are conducted in accordance with the Firm's best measure of fair value. Generally, the investments made by GP are intended to generally be private investments in the equity and debt instruments of operating companies, which do not have readily available pricing and are therefore Level 3 assets.

Fair value of these Level 3 private investments is determined by reference to public markets or private transactions or valuations for comparable companies or assets in the relevant asset class when such transaction prices are available. In the absence of a principal (public) market, GP determines the most advantageous market in which it would sell its investment. The GP generally expects to exit its investments through a sale of an underlying portfolio company. Valuations of the underlying portfolio companies are completed to compute the fair value for each class of equity and debt instrument owned by the investment vehicle. Generally, these valuations are derived by multiplying a key performance metric of the investee company's performance by the relevant valuation multiple observed for comparable companies as identified by GP from data provided by third-party sources, from transactions or from the present value of the investment's projected cash flow, as adjusted by GP for differences between the investment and the referenced comparable or other market conditions. The following methodologies generally describe the Firm's valuation methodologies.

- Private portfolio companies: To develop a range of values, which will be used as the basis for the concluded fair value, the Firm anticipates utilizing a variety of methodologies including the following:

  - Discounted cash flow ("DCF") analysis;
  - Publicly traded comparable company analysis; and
  - Precedent transaction analysis.

Each approach should be considered based on the relevant facts and circumstances and weighted appropriately, if deemed necessary. The methods used should be applied consistently in determining the fair value of an investment, unless changing circumstances make other methods more applicable. In the case of changing circumstances, the Firm will document any such deviation from the valuation methodologies utilized. The fair value of equity-like invest ments, such as a preferred interest, should consider all accumulated preference interests and other components of value based on the fair value of the portfolio company as of the measurement date. GP will consider additional inputs when it feels that such inputs are relevant or necessary to most fairly value an investment and will document the use of any additional inputs. These inputs may include the following:

- One time or nonrecurring changes or events
- Current and projected operating performance
- Third-party indication of value received as part of a sale, investment or acquisition process
- Financing transactions subsequent to the acquisition of the company
- Visibility into future material changes in the company
- An assessment of the portfolio company's management team capabilities

- During each valuation process, the Firm will consider whether an investment's value is permanently impaired or should be written off for purposes of the applicable limited partnership agreements of each fund. This may be different than an impairment or a write-down in accordance with a valuation prepared under GAAP.
- An investment's value generally will be permanently impaired or written off when its fair value is zero and has been zero for an extended period of time, the investment team believes there are no near-term prospects for recovery, and the facts and circumstances otherwise dictate that a permanent impairment or write-off is appropriate. Temporary impairments and value fluctuations generally will not be reflected in permanent write-offs. Factors to be considered by the investment team in determining whether an investment should be designated as permanently impaired or written off include the following:

- The length of time and extent to which the fair value has been zero
- The company's general financial condition and the near-term prospects for recovery
- Material adverse effects to invested equity (i.e. debt defaults resulting in equity recapitalizations, equity recapitalizations that have dilutive effect, etc.).

- Public securities: Marketable securities are generally Level 1 assets and are valued based on the closing stock price on the principal exchange on which the security trades at the end of the respective reporting period (i.e. the measurement date), unless the Firm believes that such closing stock price is not the best representation of fair value as defined under ASC 820.

- In the event the public stock price is determined in the sole discretion of the GP to not be the best representation of fair value, the valuation approach would be consistent with a private portfolio company incorporating the available stock price as an additional data point for consideration. The fair value of stock with a restriction attributable to the shares (the restriction would transfer to the market participant buyer) is measured based on the quoted price of an otherwise identical unrestricted security of the same issuer, adjusted for the effect of the restriction (e.g. lock-up discount).

- The adjustment primarily reflects a liquidity discount due to market participants' inability to readily convert the security to cash for a specified period of time. The adjustment will vary depending on the nature and duration of the restriction, the extent to which buyers are limited by the restriction and factors specific to both the security and the issuer (qualitative and quantitative). In situations where a fund holds a large position in a publicly traded security, the fair market value of the security should be based on the quoted price for the security at the reporting date, without any adjustment for concentration risk, even if the size of the fund's position exceeds the market's normal daily trading volume for that financial instrument.

- A quoted price may not be readily available for securities which trade in inactive markets, where transactions do not occur with sufficient frequency and volume to provide ongoing pricing data. Therefore, if the firm determines that the above methodologies do not reflect the fair market value of a security, the firm may apply other adjustments consistent with the ASC 820 framework.

- Other securities: The Firm's investments may comprise a variety of securities and capital structures that require additional valuation considerations. These securities should be valued consistent with the policy as set forth above. Examples of additional valuation matters that may arise on occasion include the following:

  - Interest-bearing securities: The carrying value of private interest-bearing securities should consider the underlying portfolio company's ability to service and repay debt.
  - Paid-in-kind (PIK) dividends: The carrying value of PIK dividends are accrued in accordance with the terms of the underlying security. A valu-

ation discount may be necessary depending on the health of the portfolio company and the ability to realize the underlying securities.

- Foreign currency–denominated securities: Valuations of securities denominated in currencies other than US dollars should be adjusted for changes in the spot prices of the currency as of the reporting date.
- Warrants: Warrants, like other interests, should be carried at their fair value.
- Preferred securities: The rights associated with preferred stock are generally divided into two broad categories, economic rights and control rights. Once the enterprise value of the company is determined in accordance with this policy, fair value should be determined by allocating value to shares of preferred and common stock after considering their relative economic and control rights
- Convertible securities: Convertible securities should be valued at the excess of the value of the underlying security over the conversion price as if the security was converted when the conversion feature is "in the money." If the security is not currently convertible, the use of an appropriate discount in valuing the underlying security will be considered. If the value of the underlying security is less than the conversion price, the carrying value of the convertible security should be based on the underlying company's ability to service and repay the security

Procedures

The GP's investment team will prepare an analysis of each portfolio company's operating and financial performance and outlook based on the above valuation principles on a quarterly basis. As part of this process, each investment team will prepare and provide to the Valuation Committee a written valuation analysis and recommendation for each portfolio company. These investment team presentations should summarize all data relevant to the investment team's view of the appropriate valuation of the investment at such time.

Based on these analyses, the Firm's entry multiple and an evaluation of the portfolio company's performance, GP will select an appropriate valuation statistic and apply this statistic to a normalized and, when necessary, pro forma trailing twelve months Earnings Before Interest Taxes Depreciation and Amortization ("EBITDA") to determine enterprise value of each portfolio company. The relevant Fund's equity value in a portfolio company will then be based on the fund's share of proceeds after accounting for any outstanding net debt and any outstanding senior securities and will account for any vested and in-the-money incentive equity. The investment team will then consider whether the equity value requires an adjustment based on the implied gain or loss from this analysis, taking into account any positive or negative mitigating circumstances and the overall magnitude of the implied change in value. Valuations are then brought before the Firm's Valuation Committee for approval. The Valuation Committee will review and discuss the fair values of each GP portfolio investment on a quarterly basis and accept or modify each valuation as appropriate based on the policy and methodologies set forth herein.

The Firm reserves the right to revalue a portfolio company on an as-needed basis when, in the Valuation Committee's discretion, it believes a valuation requires adjusting. To promote consistency and proper record keeping in the valuation process, all fair value evaluations and determinations should be documented. Appropriate documentation generally shall include the following: a written investment team presentation; supporting documents used in preparing the investment team presentation or otherwise used to determine fair value, including reports provided to the Firm by portfolio companies; independent valuation reports, if any; and written minutes of all Valuation Committee meetings indicating all final Valuation Committee fair value determinations.

Private Equity Operations Funding Process

Once the decision has been made to allocate capital to an underlying private equity investment, the *funding process* begins. The funding process refers to the specific procedures employed by the private equity general partner to allocate capital to underlying portfolio positions. To be clear when we are saying that the decision has been made by the investment team, we are not referring to the specific dollar amounts, the terms or the timing of the investment. Instead, we are referring to the fact that conceptually the investment team supports the idea of proceeding with the investment and now the operational procedures supporting the transfer of capital for actual funding can begin. While some of these details were likely discussed prior to the actual investment decision being made in practice specifics such as the timing and when the capital is transferred are likely finalized during the funding process.

This funding process is typically where operations first begin to become heavily involved in the investment side of the process for a new deal. Operations will first typically work with the investment team to develop a funding model for the proposed investment. This model will generally include two major parts. The first is determining the timing of the investment. The second is processing the sources of funding capital for the proposed investment. We will discuss each of these parts separately, and then analyze how they come together from an operational perspective to facilitate the transfer of capital to complete the funding and, therefore, subsequent new investment position process.

Funding Timelines

After the investment team has communicated the desire to proceed with an investment, the first question is, how much will be invested by the funds? Then the next question as outlined above is, what will be the time frame during which we will need to make the investment? Just because a GP has finally decided to allocate capital to an investment such as an underlying portfolio company, this does not mean that the funds will be transferred immediately. To begin with, the GP may decide that it is advantageous to delay the investment for a period of time, such as a month or two, depending on external market events such as declines in the opportunity set for the portfolio company which may put the GP in a better position to negotiate the amount of equity received in exchange for their investment. Additionally, the other side of the transaction receiving the investment may need some time to prepare to receive the capital. The reasons for this could include working with the GPs and external lawyers to finalize the legal documentation surrounding the transaction and providing the GP with more detailed information regarding the uses of the all or part of the funds to be received from the GP. From the GP's perspective, there is also the process involved of calling capital from investors, discussed below, that will also delay an immediate investment. In order to manage all of these contingencies, the operations department will typically work with the investment team to determine their desire timeline for the investment and then work backwards to determine how feasible this is. Then after an analysis, a rough timeline for funding would then be developed.

Capital Call Procedures

Hedge funds typically manage large groups of capital (i.e. money) that is investment from investors. Each investor's money is combined into groups of capital for different funds. The fund manager and their employees may also contribute some of their own money to managed alongside the investors capital. These groups of capital are referred to as *pools of capital*, a concept we introduced in Chap. 3. In most common hedge fund structures, money is contributed up front by investors into the fund pool and then it is managed by the fund manager.

A unique feature of private equity funds, as opposed to other alternative investment managers such as hedge funds, is that an investor who wants to give capital to a private equity fund typically only commits to make the capital commitment up front but does not immediately transfer the capital to the private equity fund. Instead, the fund manager seeks out new investment opportunities with the understanding that when they need access to it, they will call upon the investors to fund the commitments. One way to think of it is to analogize the process to when an individual is searching for a new home to purchase. Commonly, many new home buyers will go to a bank and obtain preapprovals for a mortgage up to a certain amount. This shows potential sellers and real estate professionals that the buyers are serious about buying the home and also provides the buyer with an actual dollar amount commitment of the amount of capital they have access to for a mortgage. In this case, the private equity manager is like the new home buyer and the investors providing the capital commitments are like the bank providing preapproval.

Returning to our discussion of the funding process, the role of capital calls is essential to the first major part of the funding process, namely determining the source of funding capital for the proposed investment. The operations department at a general partner will likely maintain a *capital call schedule*. This schedule will outline what capital has already been requested and funded from investors, a processing commonly referred to as *calling down capital* or a *drawdown*. The schedule will also show how much investors have on their existing capital commitments that is outstanding. To demonstrate the way this would work in practice, let us consider the example of a limited partner who committed $100 to a private equity fund. The investment period of the fund in our example will be five years and the entire term of the fund will be eight years subject to two one-year extension in the general partners consent. Let us further assume that in year one the GP called $20 from the investor. Now the capital call schedule would show that this investor has $80 left that can be called down from the original $100 commitment. This $80 is also sometimes referred to as the amount of *unfunded commitments*. Now in year two, the GP calls down an additional $35 from the investor. This would leave $45 (i.e. $80–35) in unfunded commitments. The process would continue until all of the capital has been invested or the term of the fund has expired. The GP could also call upon investors to make additional capital commitments if they find enough attractive investment opportunities to go through the original; however, in most cases the committed capital is all that is necessary to be committed. Additionally, it should be noted that the figures above are simplified for the purposes of our example but in practice there would be other items influencing the returns distributed to investors based on committed capital such as management and performance fees.

Once the operations department has prepared a capital call schedule, the next step in the process would be for investors to be notified regarding the request for capital. Historically, this *capital call notice* was likely distributed via physical mail; however, today an email request is likely more common. The notice may come directly from the GP; however, with the increased use of third-party administrators by private equity funds, the administrators are increasingly involved in preparing and distributing the capital call notices subject to oversight by the GP's operations group.

Common items included in a capital call statement include the following:

- Amount due from the limited partner
- Total amount of the capital being called across all limited partners
- The unfunded amount remaining from the LP
- Wiring instructions including specifics regarding the account numbers to which accounts should be transferred
- A summary regarding the purpose of the capital call including specifics regarding the intended investments
- Citation to any relevant sections of the limited partnership agreement or private placement memorandum (PPM) that are applicable to the capital call in question

Private Equity Compliance

As we discussed in Chap. 4, compliance has become an increasingly essential component integrated into virtually all alternative investment manager operational procedures. As the scope and the depth of compliance regulations have become increasingly complex, alternative investment managers have been devoting increased resources toward implementing and maintaining robust compliance programs. Based on the unique nature of private equity investing, there are a number of specific operational compliance challenges that have come to the forefront of private equity compliance programs.

One of the first steps in understanding the framework of successful private equity compliance programs is to understand the three different, but related, levels on which private equity compliance operates. The first is at the GP (i.e. management company) level, the second is fund-level compliance and the third is underlying portfolio company compliance as it relates to the GP.[1] Like other alternative investment managers, the bulk of private equity GPs will maintain a standard group of compliance policies and procedures summarized in materials including the fund's private placement memorandum as well as a firm-wide compliance manual and code of ethics.

At the fund level, an increasingly popular mechanism to promote investor oversight into fund-level investment and operational issues is a *Limited Partner Advisory Committee (LPAC)*. LPACs, which are also referred to simply as *advisory committees*, is a committee consisting of representatives from different LPs. The size of LPACs can vary from fund to fund and commonly only LPs that make large investments in a fund are invited to serve of the LPAC. While there is generally no regulatory requirement for an LPAC to be present, LPs increasingly prefer to have this committee in place due to the additional oversight, transparency and beneficial governance practices that LPACs can promote. The specific duties and responsibilities of LPACs vary from fund to fund. They are usually detailed in a fund's offering memorandum. In some cases, LPACs maintain the authority to approve or deny certain proposed actions by the GP, while in other instances the GP may simply be required to provide notice of intended or undertaken actions to the LPAC. Common LPAC duties can include the following:

- Overseeing and approving distributions made to LPs to offset tax liabilities. These payments are typically known as *tax distributions*.
- Reviewing or approving special situations of capital calls such as to fund additional opportunistic investments not originally contemplated during the initial capital commitment phase.
- Being notified or consulted by the GP to approve the overriding of investment restrictions outlined in the private placement memorandum. An example of the reason that this would occur would be if the PPM outlined a cap on the percentage of a portfolio that a single investment can represent. Yet for a variety of reasons, the GP may feel that going above that limit would represent a good investment opportunity.
- In the event of litigation relating to the GP, the fund terms may dictate that the GP could be advanced litigation costs to defend themselves. The LPAC may be notified of this intended draw of capital for the fund for GP-related

litigation or may be required to approve the advance of money for these defense costs.

- The LPAC would typically be notified, and in some cases may be asked to approve any proposed changes to key service providers of a fund such as its auditor or administrator.
- Voting for other changes to predetermined fund terms such as extensions of fund terms or investment periods.

Additionally, for private equity funds that do have LPACs many PPMs will contain general language outlining that the GP will consult with or seek approval from the LPAC regarding matters that it deems to be important in its discretion. This means that there may be other issues that the GP may bring to the LPACs attention that were not contemplated originally at the time of the drafting of the PPM but that may come about in the future. The reason the GP would do this is because they may feel it is a good idea to be proactively transparent with the LPAC for instances down the road that could be viewed to be potentially disadvantageous to LPs such as related party transactions and other matters relating to potential GP conflicts of interest.

Case Study

The management, accounting for and allocation of expenses within a private equity context is an area that regulators have increasingly focused on. One historical matter that illustrates this is related to a December 2008 SEC order related to NB Alternatives Advisers LLC (NBAA). When reading the following summary of background on the matter from the SEC order in the case, consider the roles operations and compliance controls and oversight played as well as what would be lessons learned and any corrective actions you would have taken[2]:

Background

9. The primary investment objective of each of the Dyal Funds is to acquire minority stakes in alternative investment management companies, such as the advisers to hedge funds and private equity funds. In exchange for its investment of capital in a given investment management company, or Partner Manager, the fund is entitled to a portion of any management fees and incentive compensation earned by that Partner Manager.

10. Each of the Dyal Funds is organized as a limited partnership and has its own advisory committee composed of certain limited partners in the applicable

Dyal Fund. An affiliate of NBAA serves as the general partner of each of the Dyal Funds and has authority to make all decisions for, and act on behalf of, the Dyal Funds. NBAA or an affiliate also serves as the investment adviser to each of the Dyal Funds.

11. The terms of each of the Dyal Funds' operations, including provisions concerning expenses, are set forth in each fund's governing documents, including a limited partnership agreement ("LPA"). The terms of the investment advisory services that NBAA or its affiliate provides to each of the Dyal Funds, and the management fee that NBAA or its affiliate receives from each of the Dyal Funds for such services, are set forth in the LPA for each of the Dyal Funds as well as in an investment management agreement ("IMA") that NBAA or its affiliate enters into with each of the Dyal Funds.

12. The LPA for each of the Dyal Funds provides that each of NBAA and the fund's general partner "shall pay the compensation costs of its investment professionals, rent and other overhead expenses of" the investment adviser and general partner.

13. The IMA for each of the Dyal Funds provides that NBAA or an affiliate will advise the fund and will "bear and be responsible for the payment of all costs and expenses associated with the performance of its services hereunder except expenses of" the funds.

14. In 2011, Neuberger established an unincorporated business unit referred to as Dyal Capital Partners ("DCP"). Consistent with the LPAs, day-to-day management of each of the Dyal Funds was delegated by the fund's general partner to DCP.

15. Certain employees of DCP handled investing activities on behalf of the Dyal Funds, including identifying potential investments by, and investors in, the Dyal Funds. This group of employees was referred to as the "Investment Team."

16. Consistent with the terms of the LPA and IMA, which specified that NBAA and/or the general partner would pay the compensation expenses of their professionals and other expenses of providing their services, Neuberger paid the compensation-related expenses of each Investment Team member.

17. A second group of DCP employees, the BSP, was established to provide advice and support, including client development, talent management, operational advisory services, and sourcing potential new investors, to the Partner Managers in which the Dyal Funds invested. The BSP was intended to increase the return on the Dyal Funds' investments by helping Partner Managers attract new capital, launch new products and optimize their operations. A substantial number of investors in the Dyal Funds also invested directly in the Partner Managers.

18. The LPA for each of the Dyal Funds disclosed that the fund would bear "the incurred fees and expenses (either actual or allocated from Neuberger Berman, or any of its Affiliates) payable relating to the utilization of the Business Services Platform in an amount not to exceed 50 basis points per annum of aggregate Commitments…" (the "BSP Expense Allocation"). The private placement memorandum ("PPM") for each of the Dyal Funds contained similar disclosures. contained similar disclosures. 4

19. A letter agreement between each of the Dyal Funds and NBAA provided that the BSP Expense Allocation would be invoiced quarterly by NBAA to the funds. B. Misallocation of BSP Expenses to the Dyal Funds

20. From 2012 through 2016, certain BSP employees did not work exclusively on providing services, advice and support to Partner Managers. Certain of those BSP employees spent a percentage of their time on tasks that assisted the investment team, such as raising capital for the Dyal Funds, as well as identifying and meeting with alternative asset management companies in which the Dyal Funds might seek to invest. While some of those tasks may have incrementally benefited the Partner Managers, they did not involve providing services, support or advice to Partner Managers in which the Dyal Funds already had invested.

21. To the extent that BSP employees spent time on tasks that did not involve providing services, support or advice to existing Partner Managers, their compensation for that time was not an "expense[]…payable relating to the utilization of the [BSP]." Instead, their compensation for that time was a general compensation expense of the Dyal Funds' advisers, for which the advisers were responsible under the LPAs and IMAs.

22. Each year from 2012 through 2016, NBAA allocated all current compensation expenses of the BSP employees to the Dyal Funds as part of the BSP Expense Allocation.[1]

23. Consistent with the disclosures in the Dyal Funds' offering documents, the BSP and its employees provided advice and support, including client development, talent management, operational advisory services, and sourcing potential new investors, to the Partner Managers in which the Dyal Funds invested. In addition, however, certain BSP employees spent a percentage of their time on tasks not related to the BSP. NBAA did not adjust the compensation expense allocated to the Dyal Funds to exclude the percentage of employees' time that was not spent providing advice or support to existing Partner Managers.

24. By virtue of the above, of the $28.7 million in expense paid by the Dyal Funds to BSP employees from 2012 through 2016, approximately $2 million, or 7%, was paid for time spent on tasks not related to the utilization of the BSP.[2] The allocation of this amount to the Dyal Funds was inconsistent with

the disclosures in the LPAs and the IMAs, which specified that the Dyal Funds would be responsible only for expenses relating to the utilization of the BSP, and not for any other expenses of NBAA or its affiliates.

[1] Current compensation expense, for purposes of this Order, refers to salary, bonus, and 401(k) contributions, each of which was expensed in the year earned by the BSP employees. In 2016, a special bonus was paid to certain members of the BSP. That special bonus was not allocated to the Dyal Funds, but rather was paid by Neuberger. While the BSP employees also earn each year a percentage of Neuberger's carried interest ("carry points"), no carried interest has yet been paid, and the ultimate value of the BSP employees' carry points is unknown.

[2] For certain employees and years, the percentage was lower or zero; for others, it was considerably higher.

Chapter Summary

This chapter discussed the unique aspects of private equity operations. We began by outlining key aspects of private equity structures and operational resource frameworks. This included a discussion of key private equity terminology including an overview of the role of the general partner. Next, we discussed private equity administration models including a comparison of self-administration and third-party administration. As part of this conversation, we outlined unique private equity administrator valuation considerations under the ASC 820 framework. Continuing our discussion of private equity valuation, we next reviewed a sample private equity valuation policy. We then discussed the private equity funding process including an overview of operations role in the developing funding timelines and in managing the capital call process. Finally, we discussed private equity operational compliance considerations including the governance role of Limited Partner Advisory Committees (LPACs) and a case study in fee management. In the next chapter, we will discuss the unique operational aspects associated with fund of funds.

Notes

1. J. Scharfman, "Private Equity Compliance: Analyzing Conflicts, Fees and Risks," September 2018, Wiley Finance.
2. United States of America Before the Securities and Exchange Commission, Investment Advisers Act of 1940 Release No. 5079/December 17, 2018, Administrative Proceeding File No. 3-18935, In the Matter of NB Alternatives Advisers, LLC Respondent.

9

Fund of Funds Operations

Introduction to Fund of Funds Operations

In Chap. 1, we introduced the concept of a fund of funds. Fund of funds are a specialized type of alternative investment fund that allocates capita to other fund managers. This is as opposed to investing directly in securities of public companies as many hedge funds do, fund of funds are investment vehicles that allocate capital to other fund managers.

The way a fund of funds works in practice is that investors allocate capital to the fund of funds manager. The fund of funds manager then divides up the pool of capital from investors and allocates it among different fund managers. The fund managers that receive this capital are commonly called *underlying managers* or *sub-advisers*.

There are two common types of fund of funds. The first is a *hedge fund of funds*, sometimes called a *fund of hedge funds*, that allocates capital underlying hedge fund managers. The second type is a *private equity fund of funds*. As the name implies, this type of fund allocates capital to underlying private equity managers. To be clear, the type of managers that are allocated by the fund of funds are not the entire underlying universe of managers in a specific alternative investment area. Therefore, a hedge fund of funds typically will not consider every hedge fund to be within its investable universe. Instead, many fund of funds seek to specialize by focusing their allocations along certain predefined investment criteria. Examples of this would be a hedge fund of funds that invests in underlying managers based in Asia, or those hedge funds that focus their investments in the technology space.

© The Author(s) 2020
J. Scharfman, *Alternative Investment Operations*,
https://doi.org/10.1007/978-3-030-46629-9_9

Operations Role in Liquidity Management

From a liquidity perspective, most of the hedge funds and private equity managers that a fund of funds allocates to are relatively illiquid as compared to public equities, for example. Investments into private equity funds are by design intended to be for long periods of time and therefore are inherently maintain relatively low liquidity. It should be noted that one reason for illiquidity among both hedge funds and private equity funds is that there has historically been a relatively thinly traded market for shares of hedge funds or private equity managers. The marketplace for the offering of shares of hedge funds and private equity investments is known as the *secondary market*. While the secondary market has grown in recent years, when an investor exists an investment early through the secondary market, it is normally frowned upon by general partners, and additionally investors are forced to sell the shares at a discount.

On the hedge fuds side, one of the primary reasons for this lack of liquidity is that they often have mechanisms in place that prevent the quick withdrawal of capital from their funds. One of the most common hedge fund tools in this regard is known as a *lockup*. A type of lockup known as a *hard lockup* prevents the withdrawal of capital from a fund for a predetermined period of time, such as one year from the time of the initial subscription, for any reason. A *soft lockup* allows the withdrawal of capital during a predetermined time window but discourages it by applying a percentage penalty to all capital withdrawals during the allotted period.

Even after the lockup period has expired, there are other mechanisms in place that delay the return of capital such as predetermined time period when capital can be redeemed. This is also called a *redemption window*. For example, a hedge fund could specify that redemption may only be made on a semiannual basis. This means that an investor can only take their capital out twice each year. Another mechanism that influences the timing of investors receiving capital back is a *notice period* that requires to provide sufficient notice to a fund manager of their intention to redeem capital prior to the redemption window coming up. Notice periods generally are in the range of 45 to 90 days.

From an operations perspective, a fund of funds manager also has to be able to meet redemption requests from their own investors. In order to do this, they must develop and maintain a thorough understanding of the timing of liquidity from their underlying investment in other fund managers. For a private equity fund of funds, the relatively long-term nature of those investments makes managing fund of funds–level liquidity more manageable. However, for hedge fund of funds the process can be more challenging. At this point, it would be helpful to demonstrate the challenge involved in this process as well as the role that operations can play in facilitating managing liquidity windows from underlying fund managers through an example.

Redemption Timeline Management Example

Consider a fund of hedge fund manager that invests $5 million each in ten different hedge funds for a total investment of $50 million. The fund of funds manager raised this $50 million from 20 different investors each of whom contributed at least $1 million each. The fund of funds investment vehicle, which we will refer to as FOHF1, L.P., has the following redemption terms:

- Lockup of any type—none
- Redemption frequency—monthly
- Redemption notice period—15 days

As you can see from the terms above, FOHF I, L.P., is a relatively liquid vehicle. Now let us turn our attention to the redemption terms of the funds to which our fund of funds vehicle is allocating to. Each hedge fund in our example has different redemption mechanisms including various types of lockup restrictions as summarized below (Table 9.1):

Table 9.1   Example Redemption Mechanisms Including Various Types of Lockup Restrictions

Fund number	Hard lockup? / Term?	Soft lockup? / Percentage penalty?	Redemption frequency (after expiry of any lockups)	Redemption notice period (once redemptions are allowed)
1	Yes. One year	No	Semiannually	90 days
2	No	Yes. 5%	Quarterly	30 days
3	No	Yes. 7.5%	Annually	120 days
4	No	No	Quarterly	45 days
5	Yes. One year	No	Semiannually	30 days

With this framework in place, we can now demonstrate some of the challenges liquidity management can pose from an operational perspective.

For example, let us say that on February 2, 20XX, an investor in FOHF I, L.P., would like to redeem an investment of $1 million from the vehicle. Remember that the fund of funds vehicle in our example allows for monthly redemptions subject to 15 days notice. Therefore, 15 days from February 2 would get us to February 17. The next available monthly redemption window after February 17 would be March, 20XX. Therefore, our fund of funds manager effectively has approximately 28 days from February 2 until March 1 to come up with the capital to fund the redemption request.

The easiest thing to do would be for the fund manager to already have the capital on hand on February 2 and simply allot it to be paid to the investor on May 1. The problem is that if the fund of funds managers set aside too much cash in anticipation of redemptions, then they are not actually investing the money but merely sitting on cash. The more likely scenario is that the fund of funds manager needs to raise some or all of this capital by redeeming capital back from the underlying hedge fund managers. In this case, the first question becomes, which managers are eligible to redeem capital from? This answer depends upon where we are in the time period since the initial investment. Fund number one, for example, has a one-year hard lockup. This means that under virtually no circumstances can capital be redeemed from the fund within the first year of investment. If we are within that one-year window, then fund number one would therefore not be a viable option. Once again depending on the relevant time period, we may also face a similar problem with fund number five, which also has a one-year hard lockup.

Out of the five funds that our fund of funds manager has allocated capital to, this leaves us with funds two, three and four as the viable options since they do not have hard lockups. From a purely financial perspective, fund four would seem to be the best option to pull capital from because it does not have a soft lockup and, therefore, no early redemption penalty. Assuming for a moment that fund four is indeed the best choice we have to then examine the redemption frequency and notice period involved. Fund four has a quarterly redemption frequency subject to a 45-day notice period.

Let us map out the timeline for fund four and see how a fund of funds operations group would need to examine the redemption process. The initial investor in our example submitted the redemption request to FOHF I, L.P., on February 2. If the fund of funds manager on that same day submitted a redemption request to fund four in the full amount of the initial request of $1 million, then we would first have to calculate when 45 days from February 2 will be. Here we are using a hypothetical year of 20XX and not accounting for things such as leap years but for our example we will say that 45 days from February 2 is March 19, 20XX. It should also be noted that here we are using a standard day convention, that is, each day on the calendar counts as one day toward our 45-day goal. Depending on the language of the underlying hedge funds' private placement memorandum, other day-counting conventions could be utilized. The most common of these would be a business day convention that would commonly exclude weekends and holidays from the overall day-count.

Returning to our example timeline, we are now at March 19, 20XX. This presents a problem for us because as we calculated above, the original $1 million redemption from FOHF I, L.P., was due on March 1, 20XX. Therefore, the 45-day redemption notice period of fund four would already put us 18 days outside of the due date to pay our redemption. Although it doesn't matter for the purposes of meeting the fund of funds redemption, if we kept going with our example of when, we could then calculate when the next available redemption period would be. Fund four has a quarterly redemption frequency. Since the first quarter of the year ends on March 31, this would be the next available redemption date. At this point, we would be 31 days outside of the May 1 deadline for the initial redemption for FOHF I, L.P.

Other Redemption Timing Considerations

While we have focused on the redemption timeline in order to meet capital requests in this example, we must also consider the investment considerations at play. Even if the timelines did work out where FOHF I, L.P., in our example could have redeemed the $1 million in time from one or several of the underlying fund managers, from an investment perspective it may not have been advisable to do so. One situation where this could be the case would be if one of the fund managers from which an eligible redemption would have worked with our timeline but the investment performance of the fund manager had been dismal and the initial investment placed by the fund of funds manager into the underlying hedge fund manager is now at a 40% loss. In this case, the fund manager would likely be better off pursuing a redemption at another fund that may be experiencing either less of a loss or a gain in investment performance, if available, rather than take the 40% loss on their initial investment.

A second situation would be during the period of a soft lockup. Under this situation, capital can be redeemed from an underlying hedge fund manager; however, this is subject to a redemption penalty. Once again, in this scenario the question becomes, is it worth the early redemption penalty to meet the fund of funds capital needs to pay their own redemptions, or would a redemption at another fund with a reduced soft lockup penalty or, even better, without the soft lockup penalty at all?

Facility Management

Due to situations outlined in the previous example, fund of hedge fund operations involve close management of liquidity and redemption issues at both the fund of funds level and the underlying hedge fund manager level. As demonstrated above, while proactive management and understanding of redemption timelines is very important both in understanding the redemption landscape and in selecting the lowest cost available redemption fund option; in all cases, the timelines for redemptions from the fund of funds vehicles themselves and the underlying hedge fund managers do not align. To prevent situations such as this, fund of funds often keep aside some pool of uninvested cash to be able to completely fulfill some amount of redemption requests.

Additionally, fund of funds will also typically have arrangements in place with lenders in order to provide financing to meet redemption requests. The common term for these arrangements are *facilities*. These credit facilities are usually prenegotiated by the fund of funds managers with lenders in advance of the need for any specific capital requirements. Once a fund of funds manager determines that they would like to take a loan from the facilities, a process also called *drawing down the facility*, the terms of the loan therefore would already be in place.

There are three general kinds of credit facilities. The first is known as a *revolving credit facility*. In practice, this arrangement is referred to under a number of different terms including "bridge financing," a borrowing facility or credit agreement. The primary purpose of a revolving credit facility is to address the redemption timeline issues we discussed in the example above. These facilities provide capital to allow the fund of funds manager to have access to capital to draw upon without having to force redemptions at underlying hedge funds subject to disadvantageous terms, or even worse simply be unable to meet redemption requests entirely. Revolving credit facilities may also be used by fund of funds managers as short-term sources of capital to meet other fund obligations as well while awaiting an influx of capital from future sources including pending subscriptions and performance fees.

The second type of facility is called a *subscription facility*. These arrangements are typically employed in a private equity context and allow for a general partner (GP) to have access to capital faster than they would if they were waiting for the capital to be called down from investors through the standard process. That is why subscription facilities are also referred to as *capital call facilities*. For most loans, including subscription facilities, the lender does not just give the loan simply based on the fund manager's promise to pay or good reputation. Typically, the lender will need some form of assurance in the form of collateral to back the loan given by the facility. For subscription facilities, this collateral typically comes in several forms including a pledge by the fund of funds to allow the lender rights to the capital calls being made by investors, either currently or in the future, until the loan is fulfilled.

To be clear, the purpose of this subscription facility is not to obviate the need for the GP to proceed with calling down capital. Rather, the purpose is for the GP to have access to the capital sooner, in order to perhaps be in a better position to take advantage of immediate investment opportunities. Then once the GP receives the called down capital from investors in the normal course of business, they then can repay the loan from the subscription facility. While subscription facilities are generally shorter term in nature, in the cases of certain investments such as real estate finance they may extend for longer periods of time to accommodate for real estate specific factors such as project development and construction financing.

In many cases, due to the specifics of a fund of fund's organizational terms, the use of a subscription facility may not be allowed. Furthermore, even when the use of a subscription facility is allowed, there may be too many restrictions in place to make their use practical. An example of this would be restrictions on the ability of the fund of funds manager to be able to pledge future capital commitments to the lending facility provider. For these reasons, the use of the third kind of credit facility, known as a *net asset value facility*, or simply NAV facility, has grown in popularity. The purpose of an NAV facility is to allow a fund of funds to not make direct cash investments into underlying fund managers but rather to purchase direct or secondary interest in underlying funds.

With each of the three main facilities, there are many different types of specific legal arrangements that may be implemented including note purchase agreements and prepaid forward sales. There are also a number of metrics often involved in determining the amount of available capital for the loan at any point in time. For NAV facilities, these metrics are based around the NAV of the fund, sometimes referred to as Eligible NAV, multiplied by predetermined interest rates. For subscription facilities, the terms used to calculate the available amount of the loan may be limited to include only capital commitments from certain types of investors, such as those with high credit ratings. There are also a wide variety of other legal and technical aspects and requirements that go into finalizing the facility arrangement. Due to these complexities, the facility loan documentation can be quite lengthy. As such, it is commonly the role of not only a fund of funds legal counsel, but also its operations staff to ensure that when planning to borrow money from a facility that all technical requirements are being met as well as that all calculations for the amount of eligible capital and interest charged are consistently calculated among the parties.

Separately Managed Account Allocations

Practically, they can be viewed as another investor in each fund that they invest in, and the fund of funds manager capital generally goes into the same pool of capital as other investors. Depending on the size of their investment into underlying managers, some fund of funds may have their capital not placed into a combined pool but rather sit in a *separately managed account*, also referred to as an *SMA*. SMAs are stand-alone structures that represent a custom account designed specifically for a single large investor. As such, SMAs are also referred to as a *fund of one* because they only have a single investor.

There are many different reasons as to why any investor, including a fund of funds, would want an SMA. Firstly, an investor may be subject to certain requirements, from either a regulatory or an internal policy perspective, that they are not allowed to make certain type of investments. The classic example of this would be a religious institution not being allowed to invest in the stock of gambling resorts or alcohol producers. If a certain fund manager's strategy includes potential exposure to these types of companies, then an SMA that adheres to the rest of managers' strategy but includes specific restrictions to these types of companies would be a good solution.

Another common reason for SMAs is that the investor prefers a certain level of additional transparency or specialized reporting that is not generally available in a similar manager-pooled capital fund. A related example to the SMA concept would be fund managers that design versions of their investment strategy that agree to adhere to certain guidelines such as environmental, social and governance (ESG) principles or comply with Sharia law. From an operations perspective, fund managers that operate SMAs for select clients often find that they are proportionally more operationally intensive as compared to the work of a pooled investment vehicle. This is often because of the high degree of customization and reporting for each client.

Fund of Funds Administration

Today, while fund of funds may still utilize a self-administration model, the bulk of them, similar to their hedge fund counterparts, utilize third-party administrators. In utilizing a third-party administrator, many fund of funds manager face many of the same issues as private equity managers when it comes to the issue of fund administration. This is especially true when the role of the administrator in valuation oversight is considered. Fund of funds do not make direct investments in equities or other liquid Level 1 or Level 2 positions under the ASC 820 framework. Instead, they make direct or secondary investments into underlying hedge funds or private equity managers. These are illiquid Level 3 positions for which an administrator would not be able to easily source observable valuation inputs. From a valuation oversight perspective therefore, the role of the third-party administrator in a fund of funds context would be to ensure that the fund of funds manager is adhering to their own valuation policies and procedures.

In regards to the fund accounting role of a fund of funds administrator, there are specific aspects of the administration process that are different as compared to both hedge fund and private equity administration. Specifically, one of the key fund accounting duties of a fund of funds administrator is to collect the underlying net asset values (NAVs) from the underlying funds to which the fund of funds allocates. These NAVs are then utilized as the components to calculate the NAV for the fund of funds itself. In practice, what typically happens is that the underlying fund manager will send out NAV performance to the fund of funds manager directly as well as copying the fund of funds administrator. From an operational perspective, it is considered to be an important part of the independence of the process for the underlying fund manager to transmit the NAV to the administrator directly, as opposed to going through the fund manager. In this way, it lessens the change of any manipulation of underlying manager performance figures by the fund manager.

In many cases, the fund manager may also distribute estimated NAV figures in advance of finalized figures. The collection of these estimated figures often allows the administrator to get a head start on their fund accounting work, and then the final calculations can be made once the final NAVs are subsequently distributed. For fund of funds in particular, the fund of funds manager is often quite aggressive in pursuing NAV estimates and finalizing figures from managers. One reason for this is that depending on the nature of the underlying managers' investments, there may be delays in calculating their own NAV. These delays set off a chain reaction that creates delays down the line for both the fund administrator and the fund of funds manager. As such, in many cases the fund of funds manager will drive laggard fund managers to send out NAV estimates in advance of finals. Additionally, the fund of funds manager themselves will also likely mirror the work of the fund administrator in-house to ensure that the proper NAV figures are utilized to avoid any discrepancies between estimated and final NAVs. When the operations group in-house at the fund of funds manager performs duplicate work to check the fund accounting work of the administrator, this is known as a *shadow accounting relationship*. These shadow relationships may also be present between administrators and their hedge fund and private equity fund clients as well.

As we introduced in Chap. 5, in addition to fund accounting, the other primary role of fund administrators is shareholder services. The same shareholder services provided to other alternative investment managers would be performed in a fund of funds context including assisting with the processing of fund of funds–level subscriptions and redemptions as well as the associated relevant anti-money laundering checks. Administrators in both fund of funds and direct alternative investment manager are increasingly involved in assisting with more expansive services in areas including compliance and tax reporting, and it is likely that this trend will continue for fund of funds in particular in the future.

Chapter Summary

This chapter discussed the unique aspects of fund of funds operations. We began by discussing the role of operations in fund of funds liquidity management. As part of this discussion, we provided an analysis of key redemption terms including "lockups" and "redemption windows." Next, we reviewed a redemption timeline management example. During the course of this example, we discussed the role of operations in managing facilities including revolving credit facilities, subscription facilities and NAV facilities. Finally, we discussed the role of separately managed accounts and administrators in fund of funds operations. In the next chapter, we will discuss the considerations for documenting and analyzing fund operations.

10

Documenting and Analyzing Fund Operations

Introduction to Operations Documentation

Throughout this book we have described a wide variety of operational practices, policies and procedures for alternative investment managers. The areas covered by these policies have ranged from investment management and trade execution through to information technology planning and compliance operations. In the course of these discussion, we have included examples of some of the documentation utilized to memorialize these policies. Examples of this have included the information security policy, compliance manual and code of ethics. In this chapter, we will first provide more detail on the purposes, goals and types of commonly developed and utilized fund documentation and alternative investment funds. We will then proceed to discuss the operational due diligence process utilized to analyze fund operations.

Purposes of Fund Operations Documentation

Regardless of the subject of the operational documentation, within an alternative investment fund documentation serves three primary purposes. The first purpose is to comply with minimum regulatory requirements. An example of this would be if a US Securities and Exchange Commission (SEC) –registered hedge fund would be covered by regulations requiring it to maintain a compliance manual. In this case, not only is there a requirement that this manual is in place but also that it adheres to certain strict technical criteria. These requirements can include mandating which topics must be addressed in the

© The Author(s) 2020
J. Scharfman, *Alternative Investment Operations*,
https://doi.org/10.1007/978-3-030-46629-9_10

compliance manual at a minimum as well as if certain specific legal and regulatory language must be contained in the manual.

The second purpose of documenting fund operations is for demonstrative purposes. Demonstrative documentation provides more of a step-by-step guide to the real-world practices actually employed at a fund. In many cases, the purpose of demonstrative documentation is to assist a fund's employees in navigating an operational process. An example of this type of documentation would be a memorandum as to how employees create a new journal entry in the firm's accounting system or a checklist of the order in which vendors should be contacted in the event of a business disruption.

The third purpose of operational documentation is to memorialize operational events. This memorialization typically takes the form of written reports. For example, on a monthly basis a hedge fund's chief compliance officer may run a report that outlines all employee personal trades submitted for a particular month or the current name of securities on the firm's restricted list in the month of March. Similarly, a private equity manager's chief financial officer may wish to see the amount of fund expenses charged in June or a comparison of capital committed versus called down for a particular investment at any point in time. The purpose of these reports is to provide a written snapshot of activity at a particular time. These reports can be utilized when called down or archived for later use. Today, with the increased ease of access to historical and more detailed operational reporting, increasing the raw operational data is the focus of memorialization as opposed to any single particular report that can be created from that data.

Operational Change Management Tracking

Once an alternative investment fund has created its initial cadre of formation documentation and supporting operational policies, this is not the end of the document production process. On the contrary, fund manager documentation may be subject to change for a number of reasons. Firstly, this change may be required due to new legislative and regulatory developments that could require either the revision of existing language or the addition of new language. Secondly, there could be changes that occur throughout the normal course of business at a fund that requires document revision. For example, as the firm grows, new positions are created and new resources and systems are added.

Firms must also make sure that documents are updated to reflect current practices in place at a fund. For example, if a fund went from being previously not SEC registered to now being SEC registered, it may now be required to conduct annual compliance training, among other requirements. However, their old compliance documentation may not reflect this new requirement and subsequently developed annual training program. By containing documentation with stale information, it defeats the three primary purposes of documentation we have outlined above and potentially exposes the firm to the threat of liability from either regulators or investors. As such, firms must take measure to ensure that documents are up-to-date to reflect new compliance policies. When a new document is created, the previous one is not destroyed. Rather the previous version is utilized as a basis to create the new document. By tracking and documenting this change management process, alternative investment fund managers can better improve their operations change management protocols.

Investor Facing Operations Documentation

Increasingly, investors of all types, including large institutions to high-networth individuals are more focused on learning more about the operational frameworks in place at the alternative investment funds to which they allocate. As part of this process, investors have developed distinct due diligence processes on both a pre-investment and a post-investment monitoring basis that is focused primarily around fund operations. This process is known as the operational due diligence ("ODD") process.

For reference, the ODD process is discussed in more detail in Chap. 11. To accommodate investors' ODD requests, as well as just demonstrate the overall strength of their operations, in recent years a strong motivator for creating a new class of investor facing operational information has developed. This could include developing presentations for investors focused solely around fund operations, or investor-friendly summaries of more lengthy and technical in-house operational procedures documentation. Additionally, as part of this process, an alternative investment fund may take elements of internal operational reports and adjust them toward producing more investor-friendly ongoing reports.

Operational Due Diligence Questionnaire

Historically, fund managers may have developed lengthy documents, commonly called *operations manuals*, that covered many different aspects of fund operations including information technology, compliance management, trade operations, fund accounting and interaction with service providers. Today the trend is not to create these lengthy manuals of this nature but instead create topic-specific procedure documents. One of the key investors facing documents that often comes out of all of these different topic-specific smaller manuals is a *due diligence questionnaire*, or DDQ. These DDQs are typically organized in question-and-answer response format to provide investors with an overview on a wealth of information about a fund management company, its personnel and the funds they manage. There are several alternative investment industry templates for DDQs put out by organizations such as the Alternative Investment Management Association (AIMA) and the Institutional Limited Partner Association (ILPA).

Similar to the construct with operations manuals, historically many fund managers would produce lengthy DDQs that covered a wide variety of mostly investment information about a fund. Over time, the amount of information on fund managers began to also include the increase in fund operations. The reasons for this are based on both increased investor focus on this area and increased fund manager resources being devoted to operations. As a result, in much the same way funds transitioned to policy-specific operational manuals, so too have fund managers increasingly moved toward developing a stand-alone questionnaire focused on fund operations. An advantage of developing a stand-alone operational due diligence questionnaire is that it usually allows the DDQ to focus in more detail on specific operational practices as opposed to providing a more general overview in larger DDQs that combine both investment and operational aspects into a single document.

While the specific questions and answers in an operational DDQ will vary among different fund managers based on applicability, there are several common areas of operations that would be considered standard to cover in an operational DDQ. These would include the areas that are summarized below:

I. Firm Overview

- Ownership:
  - Analysis of the corporate ownership of the management company and funds including ownership by any third parties and affiliated entities
- Internal capital:
  - Details of the amount and structure of the fund manager's and employees' personal investments into the firm's funds. This is sometimes referred to as the fund manager's skin in the game

- Assets under management and performance:

  - It would be considered standard to include information about the historical assets under management (AUM) and fund performance in a DDQ

- Investor base :

  - Summary of key details of a fund manager's investor base including the following:

    Details of largest investors by institution type
    Geographic breakout of investor base by country and region
    Detail of any fee-sharing arrangements with investors
    Historical investor base turnover

  - Sources of investor leads including the use of third-party marketers and any accompanying fee arrangements

- Compensation:

  - Details of base salary compensation program
  - Summary of bonus and profit-sharing arrangements

- Human capital:

  - Details of the firm's personnel including the number of people in each function including investment management, operations, risk management, information technology, legal and compliance and investor relations and business development
  - Overview of historical employee turnover including additions and departures
  - Summary of the process by which new hires are sourced and screened
  - Process for performing ongoing employee screening for existing employees such as periodic background checks
  - Details of the in-house and third-party resources that may be utilized for the management if internal human resources including workplace training, payroll and benefits administration
  - Overview of any specific familial relationships among employees that could create a conflict of interest

II. Operations

- Trading and operations:

  - Operational trade procedures ranging from the pre-trade process through to execution, settlement and reconciliation
  - Role of service providers in the trade process including brokers
  - Trade error management and responsibility assignment
  - Summary of other fund back office and accounting procedures

- Information technology:

  - Review of the firm's information technology architecture and hardware
  - Summary of key systems utilized including those for portfolio management, trade operations, fund accounting, compliance management, and business continuity and disaster recovery planning
  - Overview of any recently completed or planned technology initiatives
  - Details of the firm's information security policy including the following:

    Summary of the relevant password policies that may be employed
    Guidelines on the use of external storage devices such as CD downloads and zip drives
    Outline of physical security protocols in place including camera recordings of certain areas and restricted physical access to key locations such as server rooms
    Overview of penetration testing program including a summary of in-house versus third-party resources

- Business continuity and disaster recovery:

  - Outline of key features of the firm's business continuity and disaster recovery plan including the following:

    Which individuals are responsible for activating the plan?
    What are the procedures for making plan amendments and revisions?
    Date of last plan update as well as a summary of what changes were made

  - Details of any alternate work and disruption gathering locations
  - Overview of remote employee access plan
  - Summary of data backup, archiving and restoring procedures
  - Backup power generation, Internet and telephony plans in place

- Historical plan activations
- Details of the firm's business continuity and disaster recovery testing program including dates and outcomes of the last several most recent tests

- Operational risk management:

  - Analysis, review and testing of the controls of the firm and fund
  - Examining and providing an opinion on the suitability and adequacy of the operations for the specific strategies the manager is engaged in
  - Examine the structure of the business including staff compensation and turnover, and future business plans

- Investment risk management:

  - Summary of the ways in which independent risk management and operational functions provide oversight of key investment risk guidelines and limits

- Reporting:

  - Summary of the types of information investors will receive as part of the fund reporting process
  - Details of distribution timeline for fund information including net asset value (NAV) figures, investor letters, transparency reports, audited financials and K-1 forms

- Cash management:

  - Examination of the cash management policies and procedures of the firm and fund including the following:

    Average strategy cash levels
    Process for managing unencumbered cash
    Cash sweeping procedures including frequency
    Cash reconciliation process and frequency
    Process for managing cash movements for expenses including details of funds approvers and approval procedures employed
    Details of any collateral management and margin posting procedures
    Procedures for subscriptions and redemption management

III. Governance and Risk

- Governance:

  - Analysis of governance structures in place including the following:

    Nature and role of independent directors

Role of other committees including fund-level committees and advisory committees

Presence of other internal committees including compliance committees, information technology committees and other operational committees

- Explanation of specific terms of funds managed including the following:

  - Vehicle domiciles
  - Legal structure of funds and related vehicles
  - Identification of important parties and entities including, as applicable, the general partner and investment manager
  - Summary of fund redemption terms including redemption frequency, the presence and terms of any redemption lockups and gates as well as any other redemption suspension provisions
  - Summary of subscription terms including "subscription frequency" and "minimum initial and ongoing contribution amounts"
  - Presence of any sales charges or rebates
  - Fee summary including any management and performance fees
  - Details of any fee discounts that may be provided to groups such as employees
  - Summary of any high water marks in place
  - Summary of any tax considerations including whether the funds expect to generate tax consequences such as unrelated business taxable income (UBTI) or effectively connected income (ECI)
  - Presence of a key person clause specifying which individuals are covered, the terms that trigger a key person event and the subsequent events once a key person clause is triggered
  - Summary of any indemnification and exculpation standards such as gross negligence, willful misconduct or bad faith including which standards are applicable to which entities
  - Analysis of conflicts of interest standards and conflict management procedures
  - Summary of any power of attorney provisions
  - Analysis of the provisions and procedures for key document amendments
  - Expense management including organizational expense management, and ongoing fund expense policies including any caps

- Insurance:

  - Types and amounts of insurance coverage
  - Details of any self-coverages
  - Summary of any terminated coverage

- Valuation:

  - Details of valuation policies and procedures including in-house valuation versus third-party valuation oversight by the administrator and valuation consultants
  - Summary of the role of any in-house valuation committee
  - Guidelines on anticipated breakout of positions by ASC 820 valuation framework

- Counterparty risk:

  - Counterparty credit management by the fund
  - Funding risk analysis
  - Concentration risk
  - Analysis of counterparty arrangements and related risks including International Swaps and Derivatives Association (ISDA) terms
  - Operational procedures for onboarding new counterparties including the following:

    Initial new counterparty reviews
    Counterparty credit check process
    Formal review and votes about new prospective counterparties
    Process of negotiating counterparty agreements

  - Ongoing counterparty management and oversight
  - Best execution monitoring and reporting

- Compliance:

  - Overview of compliance management framework
  - Summary of key compliance service providers
  - Appropriateness of the structure and resources allocated to the compliance function
  - Use and activities of third-party compliance consultants
  - Conflicts of interest monitoring procedures
  - Compliance testing and surveillance program
  - Policy on the use of third-part expert and research networks
  - Overview of electronic communication archiving and monitoring policy
  - Employee personal trading policies including the following:

    Procedures for pre-clearance and post-clearance of trades
    Presence and applicable uses of restricted lists
    Use of minimum holding periods

- Program for ongoing compliance implementation and testing
- Policy regarding employees participating in outside business activities
- Presence, membership and roles of formal and informal compliance and other firm committees
- Ability of the firm to engage in soft dollar practices including the following:

  Whether the use of soft dollars falls within any safe harbors such as Section 28(e) of the Securities Exchange Act of 1934
  Recent amount of soft dollars generated as well as historical averages
  Sources and uses of soft dollars

- Legal and regulatory:

  - Analysis of the Firm's related compliance infrastructure to manage regulatory filings and adherence to other requirements
  - Use of third-party compliance consultants to assist with regulatory requirements including the performance of mock audits
  - Review of recent regulatory communication, historical examination reports and ongoing communication
  - Details of regulatory registrations of both US regulators (i.e. SEC, FINRA, CFTC/NFA) and non-US regulators
  - Disclosure of previous or current litigation or arbitration proceedings
  - Summary of any previous regulatory sanctions

IV. Service Providers

- Key service provider review:

  - Review and providing of an opinion on the quality of key fund service providers (e.g. administrators and prime brokers)
  - Review of the process by which a fund manager selects and monitors key service providers
  - Analysis and providing of an opinion on the fund's related party relationships, and potential conflicts of interest
  - Related party relationship review

- Administrator's role in valuation oversight:

  - Review and opinion on the role and independence of the administrator in the valuation process
  - Analysis of the extent to which the NAV is generated independently

- Role of other service providers in valuation including valuation consultants

Chapter Summary

This chapter discussed important considerations relating to documenting alternative investment fund operations. We began by outlining the three primary purposes of operations documentation. The role of operations documentation in meeting minimum regulatory requirements was analyzed. Next, we discussed the demonstrative and memorialization purposes of operational documentation. We then discussed the change management function of operational documentation. The chapter continued with an overview of the purposes and roles of investor facing documentation. As part of this conversation, we outlined the historical role of operations manuals and their transition to topic-specific operating policies. Finally, we discussed the preparation of alternative investment fund manager operational due diligence questionnaires and provided an overview of key areas that should be covered in these DDQs. In the next chapter, we will discuss the procedures for ongoing operations management testing, training and surveillance.

11

Ongoing Operations Management, Training, Surveillance and Testing

Introduction to Operations Training, Surveillance and Testing

In the previous chapters, we provided an overview of the development and implementation of key operations at alternative investment managers ranging from trade operations and cash through to the role of service providers and the management compliance operations. After a firm's operations have been designed, documented and put into place, they must be maintained and revised on an ongoing basis. This process of ongoing management consists of three primary operational oversight components, training, testing and surveillance (TST), which are collectively known as operations TST.

Operations Training

Initially, the focus of operations TST was on traditional back-office operational areas such as trade processing and fund accounting. As fund operations have become more complex, fund managers have devoted more efforts toward ensuring that these operations are being implemented correctly and efficiently. This is where the first part of operations TST comes into play. Training, or operations training, refers to the procedures an alternative investment fund manager undertakes to ensure that the employees of the firm are aware of how specific fund operational procedures are supposed to be implemented.

© The Author(s) 2020
J. Scharfman, *Alternative Investment Operations*,
https://doi.org/10.1007/978-3-030-46629-9_11

Training is typically first conducted when a new employee joins a firm. As part of this training, specific policies and procedures related to the new employee's specific job are usually conveyed. This is referred to as *initial training* or *new employee training*.

Three Types of Operations Training

Once an employee has been working at a firm for awhile, there are three general types of *ongoing training* that are performed. The first training may be conducted with regards to review existing operational policies on a firm-wide basis. This is referred to as *global operational review training*. Similar to an annual compliance review, the purpose of firm-wide operations training would be to inform different parts of the firm about general operational policies and procedures that may be relevant, even tangentially, to their own daily jobs. The second type of ongoing training occurs when changes are made to operational policies and procedures and the training focuses on communicating the occurrence and effect of these updates to employees. This is referred to as *operational change training*. This could either occur on a firm-wide basis or be limited to the departments and individuals that are affected by the change. One reason for these operational policy revisions could be that the firm has made its own determination for one reason or another, such as the adoption of new software for an operations function, that specific operational policies should be revised. Another reason for an operational policy or procedure change could be because of external regulatory factors that require the change. The third type of operational training would be department specific training to review existing operational procedures. This is referred to as *operational reinforcement training*.

Operational Procedures Gaps

A key reason for operational reinforcement training could be if, despite initial and subsequent training, there were deficiencies in the way operational practices were supposed to be implemented according to the firm's policies and the ways in which they were actually being performed. This difference between prescribed and actual practices is known as an *operational procedures gap*. Depending on the extent of the deviation, operational procedures gaps can serve as a drag on operational efficiency and be costly. Furthermore, the firm could be exposed to legal and regulatory liability if their operational or accompanying compliance policies described practices that were not being employed in practice. As such, fund managers are incentivized to perform this ongoing reinforcement training.

Gap analysis and reporting can be performed in a number of different format and by different groups. The first line of defense for operational gap reporting is often the individuals actually performing the operational tasks. For a variety of reasons, changes may occur between prescribed operational procedures and the way operational procedures are actually executed in the real world. An example of this would be if a hedge fund was trading in a certain type of loan which was receiving a payment outside of predetermined time periods customary for the loans normally traded by the fund, such as in the middle of the monthly as opposed to at the end of the month. For a variety of reasons, the hedge funds accounting system may not be set up properly to handle this off-cycle loan payment. In this case, rather than reprogram the whole accounting system, the frontline fund operations professional may decide that it is easier to book the loan payment in the fund accounting system as if it came in at the end of the month and then make an offsetting journal entry so that the amount and timing of the loan would be apparent. While this solves the immediate problem, there could be a number of longer-term problems that result due to the quick fix implemented.

Let us pause for a moment to consider the specificity of the firm's operations policies and procedures. In many instances, the bulk of the procedure may be written from a high-level perspective and not delve into the specific intricacies of how to perform every operations job at the hedge fund on a step-by-step basis. Secondly, even if they are detailed in nature with step-by-step instructions, they will not be able to predict every new situation that may come up in the future. In these cases, there is nothing inherently wrong with the action taken by the frontline operations employee in our example. Rather than simply let operations come to a standstill, they developed a practical workaround in order to complete the task of booking the off-cycle loan payment. Problems can develop with the implementation of this workaround as well as the subsequent follow-up.

Taking each issue separately, let us first consider the way in which the two journal entries to book the loan were performed. Following are some question to consider when evaluating this action:

- Did the employee take this action unilaterally or consult with their peers?
- Were other courses of action to solve the problem considered?

- Was this problem time-sensitive or was there time for further investigation to be conducted prior to implementing a solution?
- This problem involved the inability of the current configuration of the accounting software to handle the off-cycle loan payment. Related to this issue are the following:

    - If it was a third-party system, was the software vendor contacted to see what customization options were available to correct this problem?
    - Were colleagues at other funds who may have dealt with similar problems consulted?
    - Was the possibility of having the software customized either in-house or by external software developers considered?

- Were any industry groups consulted with regards to established operational approaches or best practices for solving this problem?
- Was approval obtained by the second line of defense, the appropriate supervisor(s) prior to the creation of the two journal entries?
- Was the issue of whether this was likely a one-time situation or if it will occur in the future consulted? If so, certain solutions may be better than others.

Next, after a solution has been selected and implemented, let us turn to the subsequent follow-up once an operational solution has been implemented. In Chap. 10, we discussed the importance and purposes of developing operational documentation. One of the purposes of documentation that we discussed was to memorialize operational events. In this case, the new problem of how to handle the off-cycle loan payment and the subsequent solution that was implemented can be considered to be an operational event. As such, the fund would be well advised to create a document to memorialize the occurrence. This memorialization would also serve to fulfill the demonstrative purpose of operational documentation by providing a future guide to as to how to deal with this exact and perhaps even similar operational problems. One of the key questions is whether the documentation of this changes something that should be put into more of a working operation manual or, instead, it requires an amendment to the firm's broader operational policies. This is something that is issue-specific depending on the nature of the operational event, its subsequent solution and overall impact on the firm.

Operations Testing and Surveillance

The purpose of operations testing is to provide an analysis of already-completed operational procedures that have been performed. This is in contrast to operations surveillance whose goal is to provide ongoing oversight of the real-time implementation and efficiency of operational procedures. In some cases, depending on the procedure in question, true real-time monitoring may not be possible but the point is that the goal for surveillance is to get as close to real time as possible. The distinction between testing and surveillance is best illustrated via an example. Consider a hedge fund that executed on average 135 trades in public equities and options on a daily basis. Prior to the execution of any trade, the firm's operational procedures require that traders log the trade details onto the firm's internal pre-trade blotter system.

If the firm wanted to see whether or not this procedure was being followed on a historical basis, operational testing could be performed. The steps in the operational testing process that we will outline in the discussion below are summarized in Fig. 11.1.

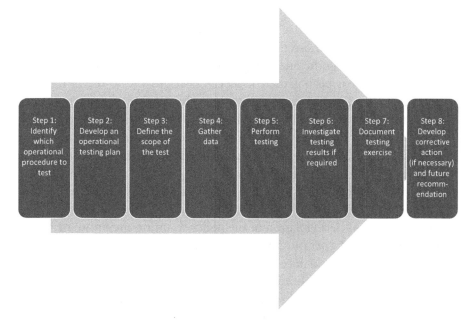

Fig. 11.1 Steps in Operational Testing Process

We have already completed the first step in determining which operational procedure to test. The second step is to develop an operational testing plan. In this case, we are looking to examine whether the all proposed trades were logged into the pre-trade blotter prior to execution. One way we could test this would be to run a report that shows us all the securities that were logged in the pre-trade blotter. We could then run another report that shows us in which securities trades were executed. We could then run a comparison of the two reports. This comparison would produce a list of any names that may have been logged in the pre-trade blotter but not executed and vice versa. We could then further investigate these exceptions and determine why they occurred.

The next step in the testing program is to define the scope of the test. For example, will we be testing the correct implementation of the prescribed use of the pre-trade blotter since the inception of the hedge fund or over a shorter time period? Furthermore, we could ask whether we will be performing this test across all investment vehicles managed by the firm or across only select ones. The next step in the testing process would be to gather data to perform the test. In this case, let us assume that we determine to examine the use of the pre-trade blotter during the previous year. To determine which data to gather, we would refer to the testing plan we developed in step two. In step two, we outlined that we would need a list of all securities logged in the pre-trade blotter and another list of those that were executed. Now we would proceed to gather this data during the one-year period specified in step three.

After this data has been gathered, we can next proceed to the fifth step in the testing process, performing the actual test. In this case, the process of performing the test would involve following the second to last part of the operational testing plan we outlined in step two, which was running a comparison between the pre-trade blotter and executed securities reports we generated in step three. After this comparison has been run, we can move to the next step in the testing process, which is to conduct further investigation of the testing results. In this case, if there were any exceptions noted between the two reports, this would be a violation of the policy to utilize the pre-trade blotter prior to execution. As per our operational testing plan developed in step two, in this sixth step we would investigate the reasons behind any exceptions noted.

After the investigation is complete, the next step in the testing program would be to document the testing exercise in its entirety including any data gathered and the testing results. The next step in the operational testing process would then be to develop a list of correct action, if necessary, and future recommendations based on the results of the test. In this case, we can consider several different scenarios that could have occurred. One situation that could have occurred is that the testing showed that the pre-trade blotter was utilized in every instance successfully, as prescribed in the firm's operational policies. In this case, the future recommendation would likely be to maintain the current procedures because no exceptions were noted.

Another situation that could have occurred is that exceptions did occur, and the pre-trade blotter was not being utilized as intended. In those cases, the firm could decide to put more frequent testing procedures in place going forward. Additionally, the firm could also determine that real-time monitoring of this was necessary. This is where operational surveillance would come into play. The firm could design automated procedures that would monitor in real time the pre-trade blotter, those securities that are being submitted for execution as well as those that have been executed. An algorithm could then be written that would compare these lists of securities and send alerts to senior operations personnel if a security was not put on the pre-trade blotter prior to being submitted for execution or actually executed.

At this point, a question may be asked regarding the point of any future testing once real-time surveillance has been implemented. One answer to this is that surveillance may not always be able to be implemented indefinitely for a variety of reasons including reasons of allocation considerations and potential process efficiency drags due to surveillance. Therefore, if surveillance is not indefinite but limited in nature, then future testing would be merited to determine whether or not operational procedures are being successfully implemented in the post-testing period.

Another consideration would be that all operational procedures cannot be monitoring in real time through surveillance. This is particularly true of operational procedures that are not entirely automated in nature but rely on more manual procedures. An example of this would be an operational procedure that would require the operations department to receive a phone call from a bank where a senior individual would give verbal authorization to release cash as a final step prior to releasing funds in excess of $10 million. Practically, there are likely not real-time procedures that a hedge fund would employ to constantly monitor whether or not these phone calls are occurring. One way that surveillance could be implemented in this case would be when a cash transfer in excess of $10 million was in process, the individual in charge of conducting the surveillance could contact the bank periodically to determine if the call had yet occurred.

Operations Testing Schedules and Frequency

When designing an operational testing program, the question of testing scope comes into consideration. In a perfect world, the implementation of every operational procedure would be surveilled in real-time simultaneous; however, as noted above that is not practical. As such, in addition to determining how to perform actual operational tests in different areas, there are two other essential questions that must be answered: First, in what order should different operational areas be tested? Second, in how frequency should these areas be tested?

In addressing the first question, we must first acknowledge the limitations of an alternative investment managers resources to perform testing. Choices must be made in order to prioritize which areas should be tested ahead of others. In order to make these decisions, alternative investment general partners typically will prioritize those operational areas that they deem to pose the greatest risks. This is referred to as an *operational risk-weighted assessment approach*. While the choice of which areas pose the greatest risks are subjective, there are certain risk areas that are viewed as more importantly contingent upon the alternative investment manager's strategy.

For example, a high-frequency trading hedge fund would likely suffer more from computer and Internet connection outages that prohibit the firm's ability to trade as compared to a private equity manager. The high-frequency manager, therefore, would likely place a higher weighting on business continuity and disaster recovery testing as compared to the private equity manager. Similarly, the private equity manager may be much more concerned than the hedge fund over the risks associated with allocating deals among their funds and, therefore, would place a higher risk weighting on operational testing related to this topic. The determination of these weights is helpful in guiding the frequency with which different areas should be tested. Low-risk-weighted items there would likely be tested less frequently while higher-risk items would be tested more frequently.

The determination of the priority and frequency of testing through risk-weighting assignments are useful inputs in guiding the development of a schedule for testing. Once a schedule has been developed, the specific timeline for testing would be outlined on a calendar. This operations testing schedule would be a schedule that would encompass department-specific testing calendars in areas such as fund accounting, compliance and information technology. This operations testing schedule is utilized to serve a guide throughout the year but is subject to change in the event of new developments. An example of such a development would be if the firm upgraded to a new accounting system throughout the year. When such a switch is made, there are a number of significant risks relating to maintaining the integrity, security and completeness of data from the prior system. The fund manager would likely view these risks as requiring more oversight and, therefore, would reorganize the operations testing schedule to include initial testing after the new installation of the system as well as more frequent ongoing testing.

Internal Audit

Up until this point in this chapter we have provided a description of compliance testing and surveillance, but we have not addressed who actually performs this testing. In most cases, testing is performed on a departmental basis. By this we mean that the marketing department would conduct testing on marketing-related operational procedures, the fund accounting group would test its own procedures and so on. Some groups such as compliance and information technology typically conduct testing not only within their own groups but on the implementation of compliance and technology throughout other areas of the firm.

In some cases, an alternative investment manager may have their own stand-alone departments responsible for performing ongoing testing and surveillance. These departments are known as internal audit functions. Historically, internal audits were typically only in place at very large alternative investment managers. Today, increasingly the compliance function and third-party service providers have overtaken the role of internal auditors; however, internal audit departments have not been completely eliminated.

Case Study

The implementation of rigorous training, testing and surveillance efforts are critical to ensure the continued implementation of consistent best practice operational policies. Compliance and operational failures can be reasons for regulatory inquiries into a firm's activities. A historical matter that illustrates this is related to a June 2019, 2008 SEC order related to Deer Park Road Management Company LP ("Deer Park"). When reading the following excerpt from the SEC order in the case, consider the roles of testing, training and surveillance in overseeing valuation operations and compliance[1]

Background

8. Deer Park primarily focuses on investments in distressed securities. According to its disclosed investment strategy, Deer Park sought to buy deeply discounted high-yielding RMBS for the flagship STS fund.

9. From 2009 through 2014, STS' returns exceeded 20% each year, and from 2009, STS did not have a losing month for over 80 consecutive months, until around October 2015. Consequently, Deer Park during this period was ranked as one of the top and "most consistent performing" hedge funds in the country.

10. During the Relevant Period, Deer Park drew many new investments into STS, and the Fund's assets under management during this period grew from several hundred million dollars to more than $1.5 billion as the Fund accumulated over 1,800 unique bonds into the STS portfolio.

A. Deer Park's Policies and Procedures Regarding Compliance with GAAP Were Not Reasonably Designed

11. The valuation policy applicable to the STS portfolio had two components. First, it provided that assets in the STS portfolio must be valued in accordance with GAAP. Second, it contained a pricing source protocol that prescribed pricing sources to be used to value the securities in the portfolio ("Pricing Source Protocol").

12. As to the first component, the valuation policy stated that Deer Park would value securities at "fair value" in accordance with Statement of Financial Accounting Standards No. 157 and subsequently in accordance with the GAAP pronouncement that superseded it, Accounting Standards Codification 820 ("ASC 820"). ASC 820 defines "fair value" as "the price that would be received to sell an asset or paid to transfer a liability in an orderly transaction between market participants at the measurement date" ("Fair Value"). ASC 820-10-35-36 provides that the methods used to measure Fair Value "shall maximize the use of relevant observable inputs and minimize the use of unobservable inputs." ASC 820-10-35-24C provides that, when market participants use models to assist in determining Fair Value those models must be calibrated to relevant observable market data, including transaction prices, to ensure they reflect current market conditions.

13. The policy lacked procedures on valuation regarding how, in the context of the specific markets relevant to the STS Fund and the specific types of inputs available to Deer Park, it should ensure consistency with the requirements of ASC 820 for the positions they valued. For example, although Deer Park relied heavily on valuation models to value the securities in the STS portfolio, Deer Park's valuation policy did not mention the calibration requirement in ASC 820,[2] and Deer Park gave no guidance or training concerning calibration. The policy also did not mention any valuation techniques or methodologies, and further lacked procedures

designed to promote consistency in valuation and to reduce the potential conflict of interest arising from the role of traders valuing securities they managed.

14. Deer Park had a Risk Management Committee ("RMC") that checked whether the Fund was in compliance with the firm's Pricing Source Protocol, which for reasons explained below was deficient. For most of the Relevant Period, the RMC consisted of Deer Park's Chief Compliance Officer, who was a former geochemist and brother-in-law of Portfolio Manager A with no relevant experience in bond valuation, its Chief Financial Officer, who is a former bookkeeper and tax accountant at a small accounting firm with no prior experience in bond valuation, and another relative of Portfolio Manager A, an attorney without expertise in bond valuation. The RMC did not have the expertise to determine whether bonds were valued in accordance with GAAP.

B. Deer Park Traders' Approach to Observable Inputs

15. Notwithstanding the design deficiencies, Deer Park's policies stated that, when valuing bonds, Deer Park traders must prioritize observable inputs such as relevant market transactions and market information over unobservable inputs such as assumptions about inputs. As stated in a Deer Park newsletter to investors discussing Deer Park's valuation practices: "Once we buy a bond at price X, X is the market price. We can't say, 'okay we bought at X but the price should really be X+20%, so it should be marked there.'"

16. Deer Park's founder and chief executive officer provided guidance to Burg and the other Deer Park traders that emphasized the importance of the requirement in the valuation policy that traders maximize observable inputs such as trade information. In June 2014, a trader and associate portfolio manager ("Trader A") suggested to mark a bond at $32.75, which had recently traded with a cover price at $37.25, because at a price of $33 "it starts to get to below 10% yield." The founder and chief executive directed the traders that "[w]ith this type of paper trail need to mark up to at least the cover. Can't be making judgments that the market is wrong. At least not in pricing."

17. For the securities in the STS portfolio not valued using a third party pricing vendor's price, which was limited to no more than 10% of STS's net asset value, every month the Deer Park traders submitted preliminary valuations, along with explanations, to Burg, who would review and adjust any marks with which he did not agree. These valuations, as adjusted by Burg, would be the final valuations used by Deer Park.

18. Throughout the Relevant Period, Deer Park had substantial access to market data and information, including trade prices or approximate "areas" in which a trade occurred, two-way bid-ask markets, bids, cover prices (the second to highest bid on a bond that traded), and offers for bonds held in the STS portfolio.[3)]

19. *Notwithstanding the valuation policy and guidance received, the traders developed an approach to valuation that, in certain instances, failed to ensure that observable inputs were maximized. The Deer Park traders received training from Burg on the monthly valuation process and on how to value securities.*

20. *For example, another trader and associate portfolio manager ("Trader B") discussed this approach in an email exchange with Pricing Vendor A, which was one of two third party pricing vendors used by Deer Park. In explaining why he did not increase his valuations in line with recent trades Deer Park executed, Trader B wrote that "we are fundamental oriented, and price them based on future cash flow ... Mkt seems to be willing to buy at lower yield,[4] which is only a technical issue, but we may sell our bonds at mkt price, only to take realized profits then rather than mark them up to book unrealized profits."*

21. *Similarly, Trader A made the following comments to a market participant regarding a CDO held by Deer Park. After the market participant questioned Deer Park's valuation in part due to a trade of the same CDO a year and a half earlier between the parties at a higher price, Trader A explained, "don't you know me at all / I don't mark stuff up / stay as conservative as possible." In response, the market participant observed, "well can't mark it lm [low-to-mid] 20s for nav / [i.e., the STS Fund's net asset value] Itll [sic] trade in the 50s."*

22. *Utilizing this approach created a risk that Deer Park would fail to maximize observable inputs such as trade prices. For example, after Trader B observed that Trader A had valued four bonds below recent Deer Park trade prices, he advised Trader A, "I think if I did this, I will mark up gradually every month at least to show we are marking towards fair value. But since they are too much undervalued, and difficult to mark up too much. So I think I will review the STS bonds to find off the mkt prices, and I will try to justify with more harsh [sic] scenario, in case auditors challenge."*

23. *The explanations in valuation spreadsheets submitted to Burg contained indications that on certain occasions the traders may not have maximized observable inputs. For example, Deer Park traders explained in valuation spreadsheets, "[w]e mark it low. it can trade much higher ..." and "undervalued, can trade low60s.... can sell it for profit if needed." In addition, the Deer Park traders' assumptions concerning the expected yield of a bond, on multiple occasions, was given priority over trading activity. Again, Burg received explanations in valuation spreadsheets, which included: "can see it trade much higher, mark up gradually for higher yield on book" and "traded lm[low-to-mid],60s [in F]eb[ruary]. but too low yield there. mark up slowly."*

C. *Policies Regarding Pricing Source Protocol Were Not Reasonably Designed*

24. *To help ensure they are marking to Fair Value in accordance with GAAP, the valuation policy for the STS Fund included the Pricing Source Protocol that*

prescribed when and how Deer Park was to use prices provided by third party pricing vendors.

25. During the Relevant Period, the Pricing Source Protocol required that, at least 90% of the portfolio be marked either at or within a defined range of prices from an external pricing source. Pursuant to the Pricing Source Protocol, for bonds that were over 25 basis points of the Fund's net asset value or NAV, Deer Park's traders priced the bonds internally and subsequently obtained a price from an external pricing source. Deer Park then calculated a band ("Price Band") around the external price plus or minus the lesser of 10% or 4 points, and compared it to the internal price determined by the Deer Park traders. If the internal price fell within the Price Band, the internal price was used. If the internal price fell outside the Price Band, then the limit of the Price Band was used. For example, if Pricing Vendor A priced a bond at $30 and the Deer Park traders internally valued it at $26, the final value for the bond would be $27, i.e., within $3 or 10% of the third party vendor's price. Beginning in January 2016, the valuation policy was revised so that bonds that had been subject to the Price Band were as of that month valued using Pricing Vendor A's prices.

26. If Deer Park disagreed with Pricing Vendor A's marks on particular bonds, Pricing Vendor A's valuation process provided Deer Park with an opportunity to challenge Pricing Vendor A's prices and request that it change its price to or near Deer Park's valuation. Burg was responsible for determining whether Deer Park would challenge a price from Pricing Vendor A.

27. Throughout the Relevant Period, the STS valuation policy allowed for smaller bonds, which were those valued at less than 25 basis points of STS's NAV, to be priced either at a valuation derived by the Deer Park Traders or an external price provided by a third party pricing vendor (not necessarily Pricing Vendor A). For these bonds, the Deer Park traders could choose whether to use their self-priced internal mark or a third party vendor's price, with a limitation that no more than 10% of STS's NAV could be self-priced by the traders. Burg was responsible for approving these selections.

28. The Pricing Source Protocol gave significant discretion to Deer Park's traders as to when to use external prices, selection of pricing sources, and when and how to challenge prices, without adequate controls to address the potential conflict of interest arising from their ability to determine the fair value assessment of a portion of the positions they manage. Further, oversight of the valuation process was inadequate to ensure consistency and that valuations conformed with GAAP. D. Deer Park's Policies and Procedures for Bonds That Were 25 Basis Points of NAV or Greater Were Not Reasonably Designed

29. As to the Price Band used through December 2015, though it placed some constraints on where Deer Park could value a bond, it did not sufficiently address the risk that the traders might value a position without maximizing observable inputs or that the traders may fail to calibrate Deer Park's model-derived valuations to trade or other market information.

30. For example, in March 2015, Deer Park sold a part of its position in the RMBS bond SASC 2006-WF1 M6 to a dealer for $56. Several days later, that dealer sought to buy more of the SASC bond from Deer Park and bid $57.50 and on March 25 increased its bid to $59, yet Deer Park declined to sell even at that higher price. For March's month-end valuation, Pricing Vendor A raised its price for this bond to $54.94 while the Deer Park traders valued the bond at $50. This resulted in a final March valuation, after being adjusted upward to the lower edge of the Price Band, of $50.94.

31. Deer Park's valuation policies and procedures offered insufficient guidance and lacked controls concerning challenges of prices from Pricing Vendor A to ensure that the challenges and prices resulting from them would maximize observable inputs. To illustrate, the following chart demonstrates Deer Park's trading and valuation of SVHE 2006-OPT5 M1:[graph available in source material]

32. As shown in this chart, Pricing Vendor A's (reflected in the chart as "PVA") initial price in February 2014 was close to Deer Park's (reflected in the chart as "DP") sale price at the end of the month; however, Trader B successfully challenged Pricing Vendor A's price downward, which resulted in a final price of $10.98, and a market value which was $2.5 million lower than its value using Pricing Vendor A's initial price. Deer Park's valuation was just under 10% below that price, which placed it within the Price Band notwithstanding that it was 31% less than the price at which Deer Park traded that same bond at the end of the same month. Trader B again successfully challenged Pricing Vendor A's price in April 2014 when it again moved its price close to Deer Park's executed trade price. On May 15, 2014, Deer Park sold $12.5 million of this bond at $15.75, then on May 20, 2014, bought a $350,000 piece of the bond – which is considered an odd lot – at $12.50.[5] After Deer Park provided Pricing Vendor A only with the trade price for the May 20 odd lot trade and not the May 15 round lot trade price of $15.75, Pricing Vendor A adjusted its price to $12.44. For May, Deer Park marked its remaining round lot position of $42.49 million at $12, which was within the Pricing Band but 24% less than its round lot trade price and also less than its odd lot trade price.

33. Deer Park provided Pricing Vendor A with information on bonds to value, including information on Deer Park purchases and sales. Due to Deer Park's lack of policies and procedures concerning communications with third party pricing vendors, the Deer Park traders, on certain occasions, conveyed inaccurate information concerning the price at which Deer Park bought or sold a bond.

34. For example, in July 2014, Deer Park bought an additional piece of the bond MSAC 2007-HE7 M2 at $29.25, yet listed a price of $21 in a column with the heading "add-on" in a spreadsheet provided to Pricing Vendor A.[6] In another example, Traders A and B conferred about what information to convey to Pricing Vendor A on another bond, and one stated that Burg "said he wants to mark it at $20, we can let [Pricing Vendor A] know we think 20 is fair." Shortly after, Deer Park submitted a price of $20 to the vendor under the heading "add-on," even though Deer Park had bought an additional piece of the bond at $27.50. Pricing Vendor A provided a final price of $20.87 for this bond.

35. As discussed above, in January 2016, Deer Park eliminated the Price Band such that, for bonds greater than 25 basis points of the Fund's NAV, there could no longer be any deviation from Pricing Vendor A's price. At that point, the updated policies and procedures, however, did not address the Deer Park traders' communications with its third party pricing vendors with regard to challenges. As of March 2017, Deer Park has provided a system-generated report of all trades, including trade prices, to Pricing Vendor A each day.

E. Deer Park's Policies and Procedures for Bonds Less Than 25 Basis Points of NAV Were Not Reasonably Designed

36. For smaller bonds, the Pricing Source Protocol afforded the Deer Park traders discretion to choose, on a monthly basis, whether to use a third party vendor's price or its own internal valuations for securities that were individually less than 25 basis points of the STS's NAV and in the aggregate up to 10% of the NAV of the portfolio. Consequently, the traders' approach in certain instances influenced the decision as to whether to use an internal valuation or a third party vendor's price.

37. For example, Deer Park bought RAMP 2006-RS1 M1 for the STS portfolio in February 2014 and valued it using a third party vendor ("Pricing Vendor B") price from February 2014 until March 2015, at which point Pricing Vendor B's price for the bond was $11.99. On April 27, 2015, Trader B received a message from a broker stating that the bond traded in the low $30s. At the end of April 2015, Pricing Vendor B raised its price on the bond to $33.50. Deer Park, however, switched the bond to internal pricing and valued it at $20. In an internal valuation spreadsheet submitted to Burg, Trader B's rationale for switching the pricing source was that the price from Pricing Vendor B was "too aggressive ... move it to internal." And again, Deer Park traders' assumptions concerning yield at times influenced the decision as to whether to value using a third party pricing source or a Deer Park trader valuation. For example, for a different bond, Burg received a justification in a valuation spreadsheet stating, "too low yield at new price, move to internal."

38. As to valuations determined by the Deer Park traders without reference to a third party vendor price, there was no meaningful check on the trading desk's valuations of the securities they traded. This led to instances in which the traders failed to maximize observable inputs or properly calibrate their model-derived price. For example, between 2013 and 2015, the traders failed to maximize observable inputs in pricing the RMBS position CMLTI 2005- OPT3 M5. Deer Park in June 2013 received a message from a broker that the cover price for this bond at an auction was $35.13, but valued the bond using an internal valuation of $12.09. In February 2014, Deer Park bid $28 to buy the bond, received market information that the bond may trade in the low to mid $40s, yet Deer Park valued the bond using an internal valuation of $11.21. In June 2014, Burg received a message from a broker that the bond was offered at $44.50, and that it traded at the offer price, but Deer Park valued the bond using an internal valuation of $20.18. Throughout this time, Burg received justifications in valuation spreadsheets for these values that included the following: "[U]ndervalued settlement bond. We can sell it for profit when needed" and "undervalued. Mark up gradually." Ultimately, in February 2015, while last marked at $31, Deer Park sold this bond for $70 realizing a gain of roughly $1.4 million. F. Burg Was a Cause of Deer Park's Failure to Implement the Requirement to Maximize the Use of Observable Inputs

39. While not formalized in the valuation policy, Deer Park's valuation process tasked Deer Park traders with valuing each internally priced position monthly and Burg with reviewing the valuation of each security and approving or adjusting the valuations as needed.

40. In carrying out that role, Burg approved valuations submitted to him by the Deer Park traders that, as described above, at times demonstrated a failure to implement the firm's valuation policy. Specifically, the traders submitted valuations to Burg along with explanations that demonstrated in certain instances the traders were not maximizing observable inputs as required by the valuation policy.

41. In addition, for up to 10% of the portfolio that Deer Park had discretion to price either by a third party pricing vendor or the Deer Park traders, Burg was responsible for selecting which source to utilize. Burg also reviewed and accepted the traders' justifications for switching pricing sources, which at times reflected an approach that did not seek to maximize observable inputs.

42. Consequently, Burg was a cause of Deer Park's failure to implement policies and procedures reasonably designed to prevent violations of the Advisers Act.

Violations

43. As a result of the conduct described above, Deer Park willfully7 violated Section 206(4) of the Advisers Act and Rule 206(4)-7 thereunder, which requires

investment advisers to adopt and implement written policies and procedures reasonably designed to prevent violations of the Advisers Act and Rules thereunder. Proof of scienter is not required to establish a violation of Section 206(4) of the Advisers Act and Rule 206(4)-7 thereunder. Burg was a cause of Deer Park's violations.

Remedial Efforts

44. In determining to accept Deer Park's Offer of Settlement, the Commission considered remedial measures undertaken by Deer Park. Prior to the entry of this Order, Deer Park hired a new Chief Compliance Officer ("CCO") with relevant expertise in compliance and valuation. Under the new CCO, Deer Park revised aspects of its valuation policy and revised its procedures so that, for example, trade information is automatically reported to its third party pricing vendors. Deer Park also created and implemented new valuation and pricing surveillance reports that include, among other things, information and analyses on challenges to third party pricing vendor prices, changes of pricing sources, and internal valuations. In addition to the RMC, the CCO reviews these reports.

Undertakings

Respondent Deer Park has undertaken to:

45. Conclude its work with an Independent Compliance Consultant ("Consultant"), whom Deer Park hired during the Commission's investigation to conduct a comprehensive review of Deer Park's policies and procedures for valuing assets in its private funds and processes for complying with GAAP in such valuations. The schedule for completion of the Consultant's work includes:

a. Within 60 days after the date of entry of this Order, Deer Park shall require the Consultant to submit a final report to Deer Park and Commission staff ("Report"). The Report shall include a description of the review performed, the conclusions reached, the Consultant's recommendations for changes in or improvements to Deer Park's policies and procedures, and a procedure for implementing the recommended changes in or improvements to those policies and procedures.

b. Within 90 days of receipt of the Report, Deer Park shall adopt all recommendations contained in the Report; provided, however, that within 30 days of Deer Park's receipt of the Report, Deer Park shall, in writing, advise the Consultant and the Commission staff of any recommendations that it considers unnecessary, unduly burdensome, impractical, or inappropriate. With respect to any such recommendation, Deer Park need not adopt that recommendation at that time but shall propose in writing an alternative policy, procedure, or system designed to achieve the same objective or purpose. As to any recommendation on which Deer Park and the Consultant do not agree, such parties shall attempt in good faith to reach an agreement within 30 days after Deer Park provides the written notice described above.

[2] *ASC 820-10-35-24C provides that, "[c]alibration ensures that the valuation technique reflects current market conditions, and it helps a reporting entity to determine whether an adjustment to the valuation technique is necessary (for example, there might be a characteristic of the asset or liability that is not captured by the valuation technique). After initial recognition, when measuring fair value using a valuation technique or techniques that use unobservable inputs, a reporting entity shall ensure that those valuation techniques reflect observable market data (for example, the price for a similar asset or liability) at the measurement date."*

[3] *RMBS do not trade on an exchange, but rather through individually negotiated transactions between an investor (such as STS) and a broker-dealer. In addition, during the Relevant Period, RMBS trades were not publicly reported and, therefore, information concerning prices at which RMBS traded was not publicly available.*

[4] *There is an inverse relationship between a bond's yield and its price*

[5] *During the Relevant Period, odd lot positions (i.e., small-sized pieces) of nonagency RMBS typically traded at a discount to related round lot positions.*

[6] *An add-on is a bond purchased by a market participant who already has an existing position in the same bond*

[7] *A willful violation of the securities laws means merely "that the person charged with the duty knows what he is doing."' Wonsover v. SEC, 205 F.3d 408, 414 (D.C. Cir. 2000) (quoting Hughes v. SEC, 174 F.2d 969, 977 (D.C. Cir. 1949)). There is no requirement that the actor "'also be aware that he is violating one of the Rules or Acts."' Id. (quoting Gearhart & Otis, Inc., v. SEC, 348 F.2d 798, 803 (D.C. Cir. 1965)).*

Chapter Summary

This chapter provided an overview of operations training, testing and surveillance. It began with a discussion of the goals and purposes. Next, we discussed different types of operations training including initial training, ongoing training, global operational review training, operational change training and operational reinforcement training. We then analyzed the role of operational procedures gaps and accompanying gap analysis. The chapter continued with an overview of the distinction between operations testing and surveillance. As part of this discussion, we outlined the steps in executing an operational testing program as well as developing operational testing schedules. Finally, we discussed the role of internal audit in ongoing operations oversight as well as a case study in valuation operations oversight. In the next chapter, we will discuss the procedures for analysis of fund operations and future trends in the space.

Note

1. United State of American Before the Securities and Exchange Commission, Investment Advisers Act of 1940, Release No. 5245 / June 4, 2019, Administrative Proceeding File No. 3-19190, In the Matter of Deer Park Road Management Company, LP and Scott E. Burg, Respondents.

12

Analysis of Fund Operations and Future Trends

Introduction to Analysis of Fund Operations Through Operational Due Diligence

The fund management business is one of partnership between asset management firms and investors. Up until this point in the book, we have focused primarily on the best practices that fund managers can implement in order to establish and maintain their operational infrastructures. In the early days of the alternative asset industry, fund investors didn't pay much attention to fund operations and, instead, the focus was on investment performance. Over time as fund operations became more complex and the risks associated with operational failures grew, both fund managers and investors began to devote more time to this subject. Historically, the pace of fund manager development of more sophisticated operations has outpaced investor interest and concerns in this area. Today this gap has been significantly narrowed and alternative investment investors are heavily focused on analyzing and monitoring fund operations during the pre-investment and post-investment due diligence through a distinct operational due diligence ("ODD") process.

Increasingly, a trend in recent years has been that alternative investment fund managers are devoting more resources toward not just developing and maintaining complex operational infrastructures, but also to explaining those operational procedures to investors. In Chap. 10, we provided an overview of stand-alone operational due diligence questionnaires that fund managers are increasingly producing to showcase their operational strengths and more

© The Author(s) 2020
J. Scharfman, *Alternative Investment Operations*,
https://doi.org/10.1007/978-3-030-46629-9_12

directly address investor ODD inquiries. In much the same way that alternative investment fund managers have embraced performing mock compliance audits to prepare for regulatory inquiries, they are increasingly focusing on mock operational due diligence audits to prepare for investor ODD inquiries. Oftentimes these mock ODD audits are performed by in-house personnel, but some alternative investment managers do engage third-party specialist consulting firms to perform these reviews as well.

A key reason for this increased focus on ODD preparedness is that the stakes are often quite high for managers during operational due diligence reviews. Generally, by the time the full ODD process begins, investors have already conducted substantial investment due diligence and the ODD review is the final step. This means that if the fund managers can successfully navigate the investor ODD process, they will most likely receive an investment from the manager. In addition to the investor due diligence efforts to date, the fund manager has likely expended a great deal of effort helping the investor to build up a level of conviction so that they will undertake the ODD process.

To be clear, we used the term "full" ODD process because oftentimes much like they do on the investment side, investors will have a number of operational screening questions for fund managers. If they cannot answer these questions satisfactorily, then the investor would consider these managers effectively un-investable because of an ODD failure. An example of such a screening question would be an institutional investor asking all potential hedge fund managers they are considering for investment if they utilize a third-party administrator? If the answer is no, this would be considered to be a deal-killer issue and the institutional investor would not need to proceed with the rest of the ODD process. When a fund manager does not receive an allocation because of operational issues, it is a disappointing defeat, a bit like tripping right before the finish line at a race.

Therefore, it is in the fund managers' best interest to ensure not only that they have best practice operations in place but that they are prepared to communicate their operational strengths and mitigate any operational weaknesses during the investor ODD review. It is consequently essential in the modern alternative investment environment for fund managers to maintain a detailed understanding of the ODD process. To facilitate this understanding, we will provide an overview of this process in the remainder of the chapter.

Who Performs Operational Due Diligence?

Different investors approach the ODD process with different resources. Some larger institutional investors maintain stand-alone operational due diligence groups. Other ODD approaches use a combination of in-house and third-party resources to provide ODD oversight. In these cases, specialty consulting firms are utilized that perform ODD reviews on behalf of investors. At other smaller investment organizations, individuals with responsibility for investment functions may also perform the ODD reviews. This is not ideal as it is considered best practice to have a dedicated ODD resource focused solely on ODD. Part of the reason for the preference for this dedicated model is because of the importance placed on the independence of the ODD function.

In many cases, the power of the operational due diligence review is reinforced by the presence of a veto function. By exercising a veto, the ODD function effectively stops an allocation to a fund manager because of operational concerns. At this point, this can be the end of the due diligence process and the manager will not receive an investment. Alternatively, a fund manager could decide to take corrective action to repair the deficiencies noted during the ODD review process. After these actions have been taken, the investor could then reevaluate and monitor the operational improvements. If satisfied that the remedial actions taken were satisfactory, then the investor could decide to make an investment with the manager at that point.

The Pre-Operational Due Diligence Processes

Pre-Due Diligence Step 1: Analysis of Other Due Diligence

The first step in the pre-due diligence process is for the individual(s) performing ODD to engage in a discussion with investment personnel to determine if there are any operational concerns as a result of the investment due diligence process. In many cases, some other forms of pre-investment due diligence may have already been performed such as legal due diligence. At this stage, it is usually very helpful toward steering the focus of the operational due diligence process if there is useful guidance that was garnered during these other due diligence processes that can be shared.

Pre-Due Diligence Step 2: Developing a Review Timeline

The second stage of the pre-due diligence process involves working with the fund manager to develop an estimated ODD review deadline. This allows the investor to manage their subscription pipeline. Additionally, this timeline allows the ODD review personnel to manage their review schedule so that we can prioritize managers in the ODD review pipeline as necessary.

Pre-Due Diligence Step 3: Constructing a Review Team

The final stage of the pre-due diligence process involves construction of a team to manage the completion of each fund manager review. Many investors leverage off the functional expertise of our different internal divisions and third-party consultants in different areas such as legal and compliance, accounting and operations, and information technology. It is considered best practice to have a dedicated team of at least two people responsible for managing the overall progression of each review.

Alternative Investment Fund Manager Operational Due Diligence Process

After the pre-due diligence process is complete, the investor operational due diligence review process begins. The investor review process consists of four stages as outlined in Fig. 12.1.

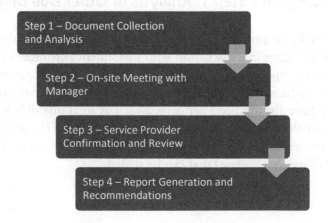

Fig. 12.1 Four-Stage Operational Due Diligence Review Process

Step 1: Document Collection and Analysis

The investor operational due diligence document collection and review process typically begins with the investor requesting a list of documents from a fund manager. These documents often cover a wide variety of operational topics, ranging from previously prepared manager marketing materials and core fund legal documentation to audited financial statements and operations process manuals. While each manager may not possess all of these documents, this initial document list serves as the starting point from which further documents may be requested once the review is underway. Additionally, it should be noted that several of the requested documents may be combined into a single document with a different name. Specifically, the initial documents requested from each fund manager will typically include the following:

For each fund under review:

1. Offering memoranda
2. Subscription documents
3. Articles of association (if applicable)
4. Limited partnership agreement (if applicable)
5. Audited financials since inception
6. Samples of recent marketing materials (pitchbook, etc.)
7. Investor letters (i.e. monthly or quarterly) for the past two years
8. Performance track record
9. Position holdings
10. Biographies of all key personnel

For the fund management company:

11. Compliance manual
12. Personal trading procedures (if not included in compliance manual)
13. Anti-money-laundering policies and procedures (if not included in compliance manual)
14. Electronic communication policy (if not included in compliance manual)
15. Organizational chart
16. Business continuity and disaster recovery plan
17. Valuation policy and procedures
18. Certificate of incorporation and/or certificate of good standing
19. Details of insurance coverage (including copies of insurance certificates)
20. Copies of all International Swaps and Derivatives Association (ISDAs)

21. Copies of all service-level agreements in place with service providers (i.e. administration agreement, vendor contracts, prime brokerage agreements etc.)

If the fund manager is SEC registered:

22. Form ADV Part 1
23. Form ADV Part 2
24. Schedule F
25. Form PF

Affiliated Fund Document Requests

It should be noted that as part of the ODD document collection process, it is considered best practice to request documents not only for any particular fund vehicle that may be under review but for all affiliated funds managed by the fund manager. A common example would be for funds organized under a master-feeder structure. If, for example, an investor was considering an investment in a fund manager's onshore vehicle, a best practice for the ODD process would typically review the legal documents and audited financial statements associated with both the offshore vehicle and master vehicle for the manager. This is done to present a more complete picture of any operational risks associated with the entire set of funds. In certain cases, risks associated with one fund (i.e. the offshore vehicle) can materially affect another affiliated vehicle (i.e. the onshore fund). Therefore, it is prudent to review all funds in a set as opposed to just focusing solely on a particular fund.

Asking the Fund Manager to Complete a Questionnaire

As part of their document request process, some investors will ask a fund manager to complete a proprietary questionnaire. It is more common practice today for an investor to start the ODD process by not typically initially request that fund manager complete a due diligence questionnaire because here are several potential problems with asking manager to complete such questionnaires as part of an operational due diligence review.Firstly, most managers already have some sort of due diligence questionnaire already created. When they are asked to complete a separate questionnaire, this creates unnecessary work for the manager and lengthens the due diligence process. Secondly, it is important for ODD analysts to be conscious of the fund manager's time and to try and not create unnecessary work for them, while still maintaining process integrity. Instead, it is preferred to perform all analysis from the ground up using existing manager documentation instead of asking the manager to complete a separate due diligence questionnaire. This results in a more authentic and detailed oriented operational due diligence review. After this fundamental bottom-up analysis has begun, specific follow-up questions can be submitted to the manager as required.

Service Provider Documentation

As part of the ODD document collection process, it is considered best practice to also collect and review documentation from fund service providers such as administrators and prime brokers during the operational due diligence process. These documents typically include the following:

- Copies of SSAE 16 (formerly known as SAS 70) or similar audit reports
- Marketing materials or due diligence questionnaire
- Copies of engagement letters and fund-level contracts
- Biographies of key personnel servicing the fund's account

Document Analysis

After the appropriate documents have been identified and collected, the next step is to perform a detailed review of each of these documents. This document review is the first stage in our analysis process and is the start of the process to:

- Assess the independence of net asset value (NAV) calculation
- Review of operations and infrastructure
- Review of regulatory and compliance

Specifically, it is considered best practice for the document analysis process, for each fund manager is a three-stage process as described below.

Stage 1: Functional Expert Review

The first stage in the ODD document review process is rooted in having individuals with core functional expertise review documents in their respective disciplines. As such, the documents for a fund manager would be divided among the team of ODD professionals, according to their functional expertise. These initial detailed reviews of the documents of each manager utilize the different ODD methodologies for each document type.

It should be noted that even though an investor may conduct separate legal due diligence, it is still considered best practice for the ODD process to undergo its own review of the legal documentation including the offering memoranda for each fund. By reviewing these documents in the context of the broader operational due diligence review, it allows the ODD analysts to be better equipped to analyze a fund manager's operational risks. Additionally, during legal and compliance review stage, the ODD team can take the opportunity to verify and independently review the fund manager's regulatory registrations.

The following is an example of a methodologies that could be utilized to review audited financial statements:

- *Audit opinion dates*—Analysis of the dates of audit opinions on a year-over-year basis to determine if audits are being produced early or late and if any lags have developed over time
- *Signing office of the auditor*—Analysis of the signing office of the auditor to determine if the auditor's location is appropriate for the fund as well as to detail any changes in audit coverage
- *Review of key sections*—Analysis to ensure both their inclusion, as appropriate, and consistency with both the fund manager's strategy and the best practice. Common section reviewed include the following:
  - Statement of assets and liabilities (aka balance sheet)
  - Statement of operations
  - Statement of changes
  - Statement of cash flows
  - Income statement
  - Schedule of investments
- *Review of notes*—Detailed review of financial statement notes including the following:

- Ownership of affiliated funds
- Fair value considerations
- Tax disclosures
- Related party transactions
- Derivative contract disclosures
- Fund commitments and contingencies
- Subsequent year-end events

- *FAS 157 levels*—Analysis of assets and liabilities line item entries and total for Levels 1, 2 and 3 for each audit year and trends among years
- *Expense reviews*—Recalculation and analysis of expenses is performed. This is done utilizing fund expense and asset information from key financial statement components to classify expenses to independently calculate and verify fund expense ratios.
- *Fee checks*—Recalculation of fees (i.e. management fee, performance fee, administration fee etc.) to check accurateness and reasonableness

After each functional expert has completed, their reviews of any additional requests for documents would then be submitted to the fund manager by ODD personnel. The reason for these additional requests often comes about because a document that was initially collected might reference another document that the fund manager may not have initially provided.

Stage 2: Project Lead Review

After all the additional documents have been collected and reviewed by functional experts, the documents are then reviewed separately by, at a minimum, both members of the fund review team consisting of the project lead and supporting lead. The two-person team conducts completely separate reviews of every document collected. By conducting a second reviewing of all documents collected, this analysis affords the ODD process a more holistic view of any latent operational risks that may be apparent from the fund manager's documents. Additionally, this additional level of review serves as a crucial element of the document review process, which compliments functional expert reviews, bringing another pair of eyes and a fresh perspective to each document.

Stage 3: 360° Team Review

The final stage of the document review process is for the functional experts and the fund manager review team to review their findings and conclusions together. This process has several benefits. Firstly, it allows for collaboration and discussion among the functional experts (i.e. the attorney who reviewed the legal documents and the accounting expert who reviewed the audited financials). Additionally, it allows the review team to gauge the functional expert's opinions regarding any firm-wide operational risk areas.

The result of this 360° team review is a finalized detailed agenda, which will be used to facilitate the on-site meeting with the fund manager. Putting in this significant work beforehand allows the ODD team to conduct a thorough and efficient on-site interview process by asking targeted questions that get to the heart of operational risks present at each fund.

Step 2: On-Site Meeting

As part of the operational due diligence process, it is considered best practice to conduct an on-site visit or with each fund manager. For a number of reasons including the costs involved with traveling for on-site visits and social distancing efforts as a result of events such as the Covid-19 Coronavirus, investors may opt to perform a remote operational due diligence review by utilizing video conferencing software; however, this is not preferred. The ODD on-site visit process consists of four main phases:

- Phase 1: Interviews
- Phase 2: On-site document review
- Phase 3: System and process walkthroughs
- Phase 4: Office tour

Each of these phases is outlined in more detailed below.

Phase 1: Interviews

During the on-site meeting, it is considered best practice for the ODD analysts to meet with the key individuals responsible for the overseeing and carrying out operational functions within the firm. When determining which individuals to meet with, the ODD analysts must consider both an individual's job title and their actual operational duties. This is particularly important for smaller firms, which only employ a few individuals who may have broad roles. At many alternative investment managers, individuals may wear multiple hats and be involved in both investment and operational activities. As such, an ODD analyst should not exclude certain individuals from the on-site interview process solely because of their involvement in nonoperational (i.e. investment) -related activities. The titles of the individuals ODD analysts typically meet with include the following:

- Chief operating officer
- Chief financial officer
- Chief compliance officer
- General counsel
- Chief technology officer

It should also be noted that it is considered best practice for the ODD analysts to attempt to "drop-down" a level. In addition to interviewing senior operations management, this process involves interviewing individuals who are often actually performing the bulk of daily operational work. For example, in addition to meeting with a chief financial officer, the ODD analysts would request to meet with a controller and fund accountant. These additional on-site interviews often provide valuable insight into the actual nuts and bolts of a firm's operational activities.

After a list of individuals with which the ODD analyst would like to meet with has been determined, the ODD analysts would then communicate to each fund manager the topics they anticipate covering during the meeting as well as a listing of the individuals they would like to meet with. This is a collaborative process and one in which the ODD analysts should actively engage with the manager in order to appropriately manage expectations. When such communication is not clear, certain managers may either be unprepared for the types and scope of questions to be asked or, alternatively, we find that some managers may attempt to hijack the on-site meeting process by making certain individuals unavailable or by not having certain documents or systems available for review. These actions may make the on-site visit less productive, and ODD analysts should avoid these issues by clearly communicating meeting expectations to the manager.

During the interview process, the purpose of these interviews is to:

- Determine a clear understanding of operational policies and segregation of duties

- Evaluate the implementation of operational practices
- Verify the description of any operational process described in the fund manager's documents
- Diagnose operational challenges and evaluate how the fund manager has attempted to deal with them
- Determine any future operational changes or improvements which the manager may face

In particular, during on-site interviews, ODD analysts should discusses the NAV calculation process with the manager as applicable. This should include a review of third-party pricing feeds as well as any internal valuation memorandum produced. The ODD analysts should then utilize this information to verify the fund NAV calculation and verification process with service providers such as the fund administrator as applicable.

Phase 2: On-Site Document Review

For a variety of reasons including confidentiality concerns, fund managers may not want to share certain documentation outside the office. It is considered best practice for ODD analysts to negotiate with managers to collect the so-called *compromise documentation* prior to the on-site visit such as a table of contents for a compliance manual. Example of the other types of documents which a fund manager may not want to send to ODD analysts in advance may include ISDAs, regulatory communications, copies of committee meeting minutes and signatory sheets for items such as cash transfers. It is considered best practice to take the time to review full versions of these documents on-site and not overlook this important step in the operational due diligence process.

Phase 3: System and process walkthroughs

During the interview process, it is considered best practice for the ODD analysts to perform operational testing in order to verify operational systems and procedures. As appropriate, the ODD analysts should ask the manager to provide documentation or evidence of the implementation of certain policies and procedures.

As an example, certain documents that the fund manager may be asked to produce are outlined in the following Table 12.1.

Table 12.1   Documents that the Fund Manager may be Asked to Produce during an Operational Due Diligence On-Site Visit

Procedure being tested	Document requested
NAV calculation independence	Third-party pricing feeds, administrator reconciliations and internal valuation memos
Compliance controls and employee personal trading	Results of any compliance testing procedures and executed preapproval clearance form
Cash transfer controls	Executed wire transfer form with appropriate signatories
Trading controls	Copy of trade confirmations from counterparties

After conducting on-site interviews, it is considered best practice for ODD analysts to leave the conference room to conduct further procedure and systems tests. These tests typically include sitting at the desks of different employees and shadowing them for a period of time as they utilize different systems and perform common operational tasks. These system demonstrations allow the ODD analysts to obtain a detailed understanding of actual system usage practices as well as determine if any redundant or manual processes are in place that poses any operational risks. Specifically, the systems typically reviewed include those for the following functions:

- Portfolio management, trading and order management
- Fund accounting
- Compliance
- Risk management

Phase 4: Office Tour

The final part of the ODD on-site visit process is to take a tour of any areas not covered during the other part of the on-site visit. This allows us to have a complete understanding of the firm's physical office space and make determinations including the following:

- If any appropriate physical barriers are in place to ensure segregation of duties and prevent inappropriate information sharing among groups
- Determine scalability of the firm's space

During the office tour, ODD analysts should also review the firm's information technology hardware on-site. This is typically stored in a server closet or similar room. Viewing the firm's on-site hardware allows the ODD analysts to assess the appropriateness and scalability of information technology infrastructure. Additionally, during this process the ODD analysts can observe whether any security or backup protocols are in place for technology including the following:

- Secure access to servers
- Cameras monitoring server room entrance
- Presence of redundant power supplies are in place
- Fire protection capabilities (i.e. sprinklers) etc.

Step 3: Service Provider Confirmation and Review

As part of the operational due diligence process, the ODD analysts should conduct a detailed review of each fund's service providers. Common service providers typically reviewed include administrators, prime brokers, custodians, auditors, legal counsel and compliance consultants. Specifically, the fund's service provider review process will follow three stages as outlined in Fig. 12.2.

A key goal of the service provider review process should be asset verification and ensuring independence in NAV calculations for the funds. The service provider review process begins with the ODD analysts independently attempting to verify the relationship between the funds and its service providers. The results of this verification process should be documented in the written operational due diligence report. As noted above, the next stage in the process is to collect and review documentation from the service provider. After the service provider document collection and review process is complete, the ODD analysts will then commonly conduct interviews with key service providers such as administrators and prime brokers. These service provider interviews should be conducted independent of the manager, to prevent the manager exerting any biases on the opinions expressed by the service provider.

Fig. 12.2   Three-Stage Service Provider Review Process

Additionally, it should be noted that it is considered best practice to take measures to speak with individuals at the service provider who work directly on the manager's account (as opposed to general salespeople from the service provider). This is particularly important for fund administrators where the ODD analysts should take measures to interview both the fund accounting and shareholder service employees that are directly involved in servicing the fund's account. These direct conversations often provide valuable insight into the actual operational processes being followed and can further highlight any operational deficiencies.

Step 4: Report Generation and Recommendations

The result of the investor operational due diligence process is typically a written report that details the operational strengths and weaknesses of each manager. This internal report can take different forms from a narrative memorandum to a more structured report. It is a relatively recent trend that many investor ODD reports also employ quantitative ratings scales. These ratings seek to assign quality assessment scores across each operational category such as compliance, information technology and NAV calculation independence as well as an overall operational quality scores to each fund manager.

Ongoing Operational Due Diligence

Once initially operational due diligence is complete, it is considered best practice for ongoing ODD to be performed. The frequency of the ongoing ODD can vary based upon a number of factors including the results of the initial ODD process, any new operational risk factors that may have emerged since the time of the completion of the initial ODD review, and the level of interaction between investment personnel and the fund manager. At a minimum, it is considered best practice that all ODD process be updated on at least an annual basis; however, as noted above, more frequent updates may be required.

The ODD update process includes revalidating the original operational risk findings and reanalyzing the firm across each operational risk area. Additionally, the update process typically includes a new on-site visit with the manager at least annually as well as an analysis of fund documentation including any newly released audited financial statements or offering memoranda supplements. Additionally, it is considered best practice to reconfirm existing service provider relationships and review any new relationships.

Future Operational Trends

As the complexity of fund operations increases across many different areas including compliance management and information technology operations, it is highly likely that the sophistication of investor operational due diligence approaches will similarly increase. Furthermore, as operations become more complex, there is a trend to further specialize the approaches taken toward managing these operational risks. These specialized approaches increasingly rely not only on the use of in-house operations personnel but also on increasingly technical third-party consultants. This is especially true in the areas of compliance and information security. Additionally, based on a continued industry-wide focus on data privacy, there will likely be continued efforts in-house both at alternative investment managers and at their service providers, on data security going forward.

Chapter Summary

This chapter provided an overview of the process by which investors analyze fund operations through the operational due diligence process and future alternative investment manager operation trends. At the beginning of this chapter, we discussed the importance of the operational due diligence process for alternative investment fund managers in securing investor capital. We then discussed which individuals and groups typically perform operational due diligence. Next, we proceeded to discuss the operational due diligence process including document collection and analysis, on-site manager meetings, service provider confirmation and review, and, finally, report generation and recommendations. Finally, we discussed future operation trends including the continued increasing complexity of fund operations and a likely focus on data privacy and security among both fund managers and their service providers.

Index[1]

[1] Note: Page numbers followed by 'n' refer to notes.

© The Author(s) 2020
J. Scharfman, *Alternative Investment Operations*,
https://doi.org/10.1007/978-3-030-46629-9